A TRILOGY

THAT EXPLAINS

Spiritual Growth

THE CURE FOR ALL
OUR WOES

JACQUELINE MCNEIL WATTS

CITI OF
BOOKS

CITIOFBOOKS, INC.
3736 Eubank NE Suite A1
Albuquerque, NM 87111-3579
www.citiofbooks.com
Hotline: 1 (877) 389-2759
Fax: 1 (505) 930-7244

Ordering Information:

Quantity sales. Special discounts are available on quantity purchases by corporations, associations, and others. For details, contact the publisher at the address above.

Printed in the United States of America.

ISBN-13:   Softcover   979-8-89391-426-9

              eBook   979-8-89391-427-6
              Hardback   979-8-89391-428-3

Library of Congress Control Number: 2024923421

TABLE OF CONTENTS

PREFACE

Many years ago, I heard the late Dr. Wayne Dyer say that there is a spiritual solution to every problem. After decades of spiritual growth, aided by meditation, service, and study, I must confess that I agree with him completely. Spiritual growth is the answer to all our problems.

On January 6, 2021, an insurrection occurred at the United States Capitol building in Washington, D.C. This was an attempt to stop the certification by Congress of the legally elected in-coming president. The proponents of the congressional party that lost the election refused to accept their defeat.

The unresolved issues of racism, white supremacy, individual rights versus the common good, disrespect for truth and integrity, and the intoxication of power led to the insurrection, which revealed how deeply divided the American people are. Many people doubt that the new president will be able to rid the country of this very negative, divisive state, and create unity in our country. I must admit that this is a tall order, but nothing is impossible. However, I believe that the solution will not be found in books, songs, or sermons. The solution resides in the heart of each of us. We must grow spiritually.

What is spiritual growth? How does one grow spiritually? It is a path of development that each individual travels. This path leads each of us from individual consciousness to unity consciousness. It leads us to the awareness that we are one with the Creator, and with all that is. The purpose of this trilogy is to help earth's humanity understand the journey of spiritual growth, which is an evolutionary process. It fills in the gaps that are not explained clearly, if at all, by some religions because this journey is ongoing. The lyrics from the hymn "Farther Along" say that we will know all about it, and we will understand why, farther along. The updates provided in this trilogy will help you to understand better as you journey farther along.

Opening Remarks

Statements to Ponder:

1. "Do unto others as you would have then do unto you."
2. God's Will will be done!
3. I am God's child. My mother/father God created me!

WHY I BOTHER

Why am I expending so much energy and spending so much time writing books and blogs about spiritual development? Do I really think that people want to read and understand this stuff? My family certainly has not encouraged me to share this information with them. They are satisfied with the limited understanding that they have received about spirituality from the teachings of traditional religions. I understand this stance because I was in this position a few decades ago.

In 1985, my long-accepted understanding of religious teachings began to change. This change was ignited by the demonstration of changes that were taking place in me. I was progressing in evolution, and this progress was being shown to me by phenomena such as hearing voices, seeing clairvoyantly, having visitations with family and friends who had passed over, leaving my physical body and visiting other dimensions, and feeling giant waves of energy moving throughout my physical body. This was all new to me and I wanted to understand what and why this was happening. At this time, I began to seek, and I did find.

I write to share my findings with others. When I first began to understand spiritual growth or evolution of consciousness, I was not pleased that none of my many years of religious training had prepared me for what I was learning. Since I would have liked to have learned this information at an earlier age, I decided that I would share what I was learning with others. I would do unto others as I would have wanted others to do unto me. Please know that I am not trying to convince anyone to change their religion. I simply want people to be aware that there is more to know about spirituality. As we evolve, things change. Master Saint Germain said in his book on alchemy: "We all have a responsibility to encourage the light to expand in all people, but each one must open the door for himself."

By sharing my writings, I have accepted the responsibility to encourage the light to expand in others. However, I know that I cannot force others to learn what spiritual growth is, and what they can do to help themselves to advance more quickly in evolution. That's a task that each individual must either accept or reject. However, they cannot accept or reject this task if they do not know that this option exists. My writings can make the readers aware of this option.

I must also admit that this time in which we are now living is difficult. The effects of climate change are destroying homes, food crops, and communities. A global pandemic is taking many lives. Racism is still a huge problem, and lack of affordable healthcare and poverty are increasing in the United States. Many Americans see much darkness and very little light in their lives. As for me, I always say: God's Will will be done. I think and say this often. Master Saint Germain agrees with me. In his book on alchemy, he says: "Anxiety must be replaced by faith and solemn confidence in the outworking of the divine plan." I know that as we grow spiritually, we become better equipped to co-create with God. Eventually, we will let go and let God rule all that we say and do. I believe this, and this is why I bother to write and share my writings with you.

Jackie Watts

Statements to Ponder:

1. Everything must change. Nothing stays the same.

2. We are growing spiritually. We are evolving.

3. Spirit is energy. Spirit is all that is.

Blog 1

EVOLUTION

Everything must change. Nothing stays the same. These are the lyrics of a well-known gospel song. Webster's Dictionary defines evolution as follows: "Any process of change or growth." "A process of change in a particular direction." "A theory that the various kinds of plants and animals are descended from other kinds that lived in earlier times and that the differences are due to inherited changes that occurred over many generations." Synonyms for the word "evolution" are *development, elaboration, expansion, growth, progress, and progression.*

I totally agree with the first two definitions, and also with the synonyms given. However, the third definition describes what we know as Darwin's theory of evolution, and although I personally believe it is true, in this blog I am addressing the evolution of consciousness (awareness) in human beings. Consciousness pertains to energy or spirit. The frequency of energy determines how light or heavy an object is. This applies to everything that exists, minerals as well as plants and animals. Over time, minerals can evolve into sparkling stones. Carbon changing into diamonds is an example of this. Human beings also evolve. The thinking patterns and the character traits of humans in ancient times are different from those of humans today.

In the Bible, Jesus, a very evolved human being, is credited with providing the teachings in the New Testament. He is shown in many pictures to have a ring of light around his head. This ring of light represents his spiritual growth. It shows that his physical body has become less dense. The transfiguration story in Mark, chapter 9, also expresses this concept. Like the evolved mineral, the diamond, Jesus's body is radiating light. The story of Jesus applies to all mankind. It illustrates that we evolve from human beings to spirit beings. Our carbon based bodies become crystalline-based, and we become more aware of things that were at one time invisible to us. Becoming spirit beings is the next step in evolution for mankind. Like Jesus, and everything else that exists, we are changing. We are not staying the same.

Statements to Ponder:

1. God is the source of all creation
2. God is transcendent and immanent. God is both near and far.
3. Like God, I am Divine.

Blog 2

What / Who is God?

According to John 4:24 in the Bible's New Testament, God is a Spirit who must be worshipped in spirit and in truth. Isaiah 44:6 says that God is the first, and the last, and besides him there is no God. Ephesians 4:6 says that there is one God and Father of all, who is above all, and through all, and in all. 1 John1:15 describes God's perfection by saying: "God is light, and in him is no darkness at all." In the Bhagavad Gita, Krishna says that the Spirit, (which is God), pervades the entire universe and is indestructible. It is neither born nor does it die at any time. Most important, Genesis 1:27 says that man is made in the image of God.

There are many other verses and sayings that echo the ideas expressed about God in the previous paragraph. The teachings of the Ageless Wisdom / Esoteric Philosophy concur in that they proclaim that God was first to exist, and from God everything else was created, including man. These teachings also explain how man, who is made in the image of God, is spirit, just like God. In addition, we learn from the Esoteric Philosophy, how the energies of God, called the seven rays, descended from afar over millions, perhaps billions of years, to create the mineral, plant, and animal kingdoms, and lastly to create man. After the creation of Adam, the first man according to the Bible, the human kingdom grew and progressed through a protracted evolutionary process which is still ongoing today. As mankind proceeds in evolution, one day, like Jesus, our energy frequency will be raised sufficiently, and we will ascend. At that time, each of us will realize that our dense physical body was an illusion. We are spirit, and like God, we are divine.

Statements to Ponder:

1. "If you knew me, you would know my Father also." (John 8:14)

2. "I and the Father are One." (John 10:30)

3. We are all one.

Blog 3

RELIGION AND SPIRITUALITY

I have heard many people say that they are not religious, but they are spiritual. What does this mean?

Webster's Dictionary defines *religion* as follows:

- A cause, principle, or belief held to with faith and ardor.

- A specific fundamental set of beliefs and practices generally agreed upon by a number of persons or sects.

- Devotion to a religious faith.

- Synonyms: Devotion, Faith, Piety, Creed, Persuasion

On the other hand, it defines *spirituality* as:

- Of, relating to, consisting of, or affecting the spirit.

- Incorporeal, as distinguished from the physical nature.

- Synonyms: Bodiless, Immaterial, Nonphysical, Religious, Devotional

Speaking for myself, I have been both religious and spiritual. However, at this stage in my life, I am much more spiritual than religious. I will explain, but before doing so, I must share the following verses from the Bible's New Testament with you:

- "There is a natural body, and there is a spiritual body." (1 Cor. 15:44)

- "Flesh and blood cannot inherit the kingdom of God." (1 Cor. 15:50)

- "As many as are led by the Spirit of God, they are the sons of God." (Romans 8:14)

- "It is the spirit that gives life, the flesh is of no avail; the words that I have spoken to you are spirit and life." (John 6:63)

- "Truly, truly I say to you, unless one is born of water and the Spirit he cannot enter the kingdom of God. That which is born of the flesh is flesh, and that which is born of the Spirit is spirit. Do not marvel that I said to you, 'You must be born anew'." (John 3:5-7)

These Bible verses express what I know to be true, but my understanding of them is not based on what I was taught in the churches of traditional religions. My understanding is based on the supernatural phenomena that I personally experienced, and on my arduous seeking to understand them. Paraphrasing Matthew 7:7-8, I asked and it was given me, I sought and I found, I knocked and it was opened to me.

Today, I understand that to be born anew, my physical body must be purified totally by ridding it of the lower, negative energies that I created or somehow acquired during many lifetimes. Doing this will allow my higher, spiritual body to resurface and take control of my life. This is accomplished by the evolutionary process that I mentioned in my first two blogs, and explained in more details in my book Spirit Answers. When the physical self is purified, and the spiritual self is in control, we become Spirit Beings. Then, we are able to understand how we are One with God, and with all that is.

Statements to Ponder:

1. "Behold, a virgin shall conceive, and bear a son, and shall call his name Immanuel." (Isaiah 7:14)

2. "Thou shalt call his name Jesus: For he shall save his people from their sins." (Matthews 1:21)

Blog 4

JESUS – Part I

While chatting with my sister, I became aware that her understanding of Jesus, the main character in the Bible's New Testament, is somewhat different from mine. Since the religion, Christianity, is based on the teachings of Jesus, and a large part of earth's humanity is Christian, I decided to write this blog and several additional ones to share my understanding of this incredible teacher.

Who is this man that we call Jesus? People say that he is the only son of God. They also say that he saved humankind from sin. Is this true, or has Jesus's nature and purpose been misunderstood?

The Christian world celebrates December 25th as a holiday called Christmas. This is Jesus's birthday. He was born in a manger in Bethlehem. His mother had become pregnant without having sex with a man. She was called "The Virgin Mary". His father, Joseph, a carpenter, was convinced by the angel Gabriel that Mary had not cheated on him. Joseph married Mary and became the earth father to Jesus, God's only son.

As a child, Jesus had an exceptional interest in spiritual truths. He engaged in discussions with religious authorities at a young age, when most boys would have been playing games with other kids. At the age of twelve, he disappeared from biblical scriptures and did not reappear until age thirty. At that age, he gathered a group of twelve men and went from town to town teaching spiritual truths to anyone who would listen. Jesus demonstrated mastery of alchemy and spiritual laws by performing feats such as waking the dead, healing the sick, turning water into wine, giving sight to the blind, ordering the wind and the waves to be still, and walking on water.

The rest of Jesus' biography is well-known by the Christian world. He was arrested, tried, and convicted of sedition (treason), and crucified. He died on a cross, was buried in a cave, arose from his grave, and appeared to his disciples. After Jesus departed, his disciples and followers went throughout the world teaching what Jesus had taught them. From these activities, the religion Christianity was created. Now, more than two thousand years later, Christianity is the religion of choice of millions, perhaps billions, of people throughout planet Earth.

Having read this blog, do you really know Jesus? There is much more to learn. You will know him better as you continue to read these blogs.

Statements to Ponder:

1. "He taught them as one that had authority." (Mark 1:22)

2. "Let that mind be in me that was in Christ Jesus." (Philippians 2:5)

3. "I can do all things through Christ who strengthens me." (Philippians 4:13)

4. "There is...one mediator between God and men, the man Christ Jesus." (1 Timothy 2:5)

Blog 5

JESUS – Part 2

Many people call him Jesus Christ, but we know that Christ was not his last name. The Bible often refers to him as Christ Jesus. I have also heard him called Jesus, the Christ. What's the deal with this "Christ" reference?

According to the Ageless Wisdom/Esoteric Philosophy teachings, Christ represents the middle principle which is the Christ consciousness in man. Huh? Let me back up and set forth the bible verse found in 1 Timothy 2:5 – "There is...one mediator between God and men, the man Christ Jesus." To understand this verse, you must know that there are three levels of consciousness in every human being. The lowest level is the ego or personality self, which is where the majority of earth's humanity is and has been for many, many years. At this level, we believe that our physical body is all that we are. Many of us do not realize that we are also composed of levels of energy that are less dense and vibrate at a more rapid speed than our lower physical body. As we raise ourselves into higher levels of energy, our awareness and our powers increase.

As we evolve from the lower, ego level, we raise our consciousness/awareness to the second level. This level is the

Christ consciousness or middle level. It is also called the higher self, or the Soul. Jesus attained this level of consciousness. He was called "Christ" because he exhibited the Christ consciousness. This explains why he could perform what were called "miracles" by lesser evolved men. At this level of evolution, the Christ Self (Soul) receives information and guidance directly from its individualized God (I Am Presence), or highest self. When we receive and obey this guidance, which is passed down to the ego (personality self) via the Soul, we are doing God's will, which is free of sin. Please understand that in order for us to receive guidance from these higher sources, our consciousness must be raised. We must have grown spiritually. (To understand this spiritual growth process, please read about the initiations discussed in my book Spirit Answers.)

The highest level of awareness in man is the God consciousness or the I Am Presence. The Christ consciousness is the mediator between the higher God consciousness and the lower ego consciousness. In other words, it connects our lower ego self to our highest God self. Because of this connection, Jesus knew that he and the Father were one.

Statements to Ponder:

1. "Christ in me the hope of glory." (Colossians 1:27)

2. "Is it not written in your law, 'I said, ye are Gods'?" (John 10:34)

3. "Verily, verily I say to you, he that believeth on me, the works that I do shall he do also, and greater works than these shall he do, because I go to my Father." (John 14:12)

Blog 6

JESUS – Part 3

In blogs four and five, we were told that Jesus was more advanced in evolution than most of planet earth's humanity. Why was his evolution more advanced? What did he do to raise his consciousness so much more than the rest of us?

Firstly, there is the factor of reincarnation, which is the subject of my book entitled Glimpses of a Life. We can assume that during his many embodiments, Jesus' actions and words were for the most part compatible with the higher energies of his I AM Presence. In other words, he did not fill his lower ego body with heavy, dense energies which we would call sins. Furthermore, in time, he transmuted the dense energies that he had accumulated in his lower body, if he did commit sins, and by doing so, he raised his consciousness.

Secondly, how did Jesus know how to transmute the lower, heavy energies that he had accumulated in his ego self? Do you remember that Jesus disappeared from biblical scripture for eighteen years? Reliable sources attest that Jesus spent those years in India, Tibet, and Nepal. He went there to perfect himself in the Divine Word and to study spiritual laws. While in the East, Jesus prayed, meditated, practiced yoga, studied, and taught. He mastered spiritual laws and the art of alchemy. He believed in the injunction: "Know Thyself", and he pursued a path of self-mastery, not as a god, but on a course of soul-evolution which is obtainable by all. On returning to Israel, Jesus' desire was not to start a religion. He launched a public ministry to show others how to grow spiritually more quickly. Jesus wanted to share what he had learned. He wanted us to know that life is everlasting, we are all one with God, and because of our God connection, we have unlimited powers. He said: "I am the way, the truth, and the life. Come follow me." We only need to believe Jesus and follow him, as he commanded.

Whether or not we learned what Jesus taught is debatable, especially since many of us have not yet made the resurrection and ascension that he demonstrated.

Statements to Ponder:

1. "God is love." (1 John 4:16)

2. "If we love one another, God dwelleth in us, and his love is perfected in us." (1 John 4:12)

3. "Hatred stirreth up strifes: but love covereth all sins." (Proverbs 10:12)

Blog 7

JESUS – PART 4

Jesus' teachings can be summed up in one word: LOVE. Everything is energy/spirit. God is an energy/spirit entity. God is love. Love is a divine energy. It radiates at the highest frequency possible. The light and vibrational frequency of love makes God all-powerful, all-knowing, and everywhere present. God's possessions are unlimited. This is why the Bible tells us: "Seek ye first the kingdom of God and his righteousness, and all these things shall be yours as well." (Matthew 6:33) The kingdom of God is Divine Love. When our evolutionary path leads us back to the fullness of God, or source energy, we will regain the power and abilities that we had before our consciousness descended into lower dimensions. The Bible describes this descent or involution as The Fall, or the Adam and Eve story. When we evolve, we raise our consciousness and reverse the descent of The Fall.

The Bible is loaded with verses about love. Some of them are:

1. "God is love." (1 John 4:16)

2. "Love is the fulfilling of the law." (Romans 13:10)

3. "God hath not given us the spirit of fear, but of power and love." (2 Timothy 1:7)

4. "Thy shalt love thy neighbor as thyself." (Leviticus 19:18)

5. "By love serve one another." (Galatians 5:13)

6. "Many waters cannot quench love, neither can the floods drown it." (Song of Solomon 8:7)

7. "My little children, let us not love in word, neither in tongue; but in deed and in truth." (1 John 3:18)

8. "Every one that loveth is born of God." (1 John 4:7)

9. "Perfect love casteth out fear." (1 John 4:18)

10. "Keep yourselves in the love of God." (Jude 1:21)

When we are functioning in the love of God, all things are perfect. Love is indeed the answer. The love that we radiate at times from the level of our lower ego consciousness will, as we evolve, eventually lead us to radiate full-time the greater love of the soul and of God. Like Jesus, we will be resurrected and we will ascend. Then, we will dwell in the Kingdom of God.

Statements to Ponder:

1. "Work out your own salvation with fear and trembling." (Phil. 2:12)

2. "Every man shall bear his own burden." (Gal. 6:5)

3. If anyone keeps my word, he will never see death." (John 8:51)

Blog 8

JESUS – PART 5

Jesus said that in order to gain salvation and thereby become free, we must follow him. What does it mean to follow him? Many people believe that to say that they accept Jesus as their savior gives them salvation. All they have to do is to say that they accept Jesus's words and be baptized. This frees them of sin. For me, this is only the first step.

To follow Jesus means that we must do as he did. We must study and understand his word, and we must keep it. The bible verse John 8:51 says: "If anyone keeps my word, he will never see death." John 8, verses 31 and 32 read as follows: "Jesus then said to the Jews who had believed in him, 'If you continue in my word, you are truly my disciples, and you will know the truth, and the truth will make you free'."

In her book: The Lost Teachings of Jesus Vol. 4, Elizabeth Clare Prophet explains clearly what it means to keep Jesus's words. She says: "The words of Jesus won't help you a bit unless you listen to them, understand them, and heed them." She also says, : " Unless we can do the things that Christ did, we're not going to be regenerated. And we can start whenever we want to. It doesn't matter what church or synagogue you belong to or what doctrine you believe. It's the Truth that will make you free – if you know it, and if you do it."

To me, the key words offered by Elizabeth Prophet are <u>heed</u> and <u>do</u>. She understood that salvation must be worked out. This idea returns us to the understanding that *we must grow spiritually*. We must raise our consciousness in order to evolve from our lower ego self to our higher Christ consciousness self. Thus, we will be born again. We will be regenerated. **We follow Jesus by doing what he did**. Thus, we will be saved.

Statements to Ponder:

1. You reap what you sow.

2. What goes around comes around.

3. The Law of Cause and Effect

Blog 9

KARMA and REINCARNATION

In previous blogs, I stated that humankind resulted when the highest divine energies (known as the seven rays), descended into lower planes. The strongest three rays are called *The Trinity*, and the remaining four rays are offshoots of ray three. All seven rays have unique qualities and they are the source of everything that is created. They are source energy, creator of all, or God.

As a result of the descent (involution), and the evolutionary process, the powers of the seven rays in man are greatly reduced from their initial potency as source energy. Man has lost the full power of his connection with God. This is explained in the Christian bible as *The Fall*, or the Adam and Eve story. Man, who now resides in his lower physical body, is being guided by his ego or personality self rather than by his higher soul and highest God self. Unfortunately, the lower personality self does not always make wise choices based in love. As a result of these ungodly choices, that we call sins, man has allowed heavy, negative energies to enter into our lower body system. These negative energies cling to us and we must rid ourselves of them in order for our evolution in consciousness to proceed. This clinging of energies is called karma. Whatever wrong we do comes back to us for resolution. We reap what we sow.

The resolving of karmic debts does not always take place quickly. Sometimes it takes many lifetimes for our systems to purify themselves of the negative energies that they have created due to their choices that were not based in love. Since we were not given a free pass to the next step in evolution, our souls had to reembody many times until we learned important lessons and paid our karmic debts. This re-entrance of the soul into new physical bodies after dying in previous ones is called reincarnation. I think of it as the soul or higher self being given another opportunity to purify its lower body system. By doing so, we release our lower, negative energies and allow our lower personality self to rise up and be regenerated or born again. This done, the soul or higher self becomes dominate and it guides our choices. Then we can proceed with the evolutionary process.

When our lower (personality self) and higher bodies (soul) become one hundred percent pure, we ascend and become spirit beings. We have no more need for a lower physical body. Having completed its job, the soul disappears and we become one with our highest self, also known as our I AM Presence or individualized God self.

My book, Glimpses of a Life, is a true fantasy story that illustrates the reincarnation process. Using past life regressions, ageless wisdom truths, and my spirit-fed imagination, I described my life from prehistorical times to the present. I ended the story by revealing what the future holds for all of us. Glimpses of a Life can clarify one's understanding of life as a human being. I highly recommend it (smile).

Hopefully, this blog has helped you to realize that man plays a major role in determining his fate. Our thoughts, feelings, words and actions make us who we are and who we become.

Statements to Ponder:

1. "Thou shalt make thy prayer unto him and he shall hear thee." (Job 22:27)

2. "Be still and know that I am God." (Psalm 46:10)

Blog 10

PRAYER AND MEDITATION

Have you wondered why religions in the western world encourage their congregants to pray, whereas eastern world religions such as Buddhism and Hinduism emphasize the practice of meditation? Why is this so, and what is the difference between prayer and meditation?

I will begin offering my understanding of how they differ by sharing the synonyms given in Webster's dictionary:

- Prayer – entreat, supplicate, beg, beseech, implore
- Meditate – ponder, muse, study, think, contemplate, plan, devise

In my opinion, both prayer and meditation are means of communicating with one's I AM Presence/ Individualized God/ Highest Self. However, the level of the communication is different. Many people who are advanced in evolution say that by praying, one speaks to God. Many of our prayers are petitions for health, wealth, and protection for ourselves and our loved ones. In our prayers we also offer praise and give thanks to our creator for blessing us. To facilitate the process of praying, many of us recite prayers that we have memorized such as *The Lord's Prayer* which is offered in the bible. Others compose their prayers according to what is currently transpiring in their lives and in the world.

Speaking to God is a helpful activity if God needs for us to tell Him what is transpiring in our lives, and what our needs are. Since God is omniscient (all-knowing), it seems to me that He always knows our needs. Nevertheless, it doesn't hurt to praise Him and to remind Him that we are counting on His help. But, do we always know God's response to us? Do we listen and receive God's guidance? This is where meditation fits into the picture of communicating with God.

When we pray, we talk to God. Whereas, meditation helps us to hear God clearly. By meditating in the silence, we are able to remove negative energies that block the flow of higher source energies into our lower body. Meditation helps us to open these blocked channels. By doing so, our consciousness is raised to a higher frequency.

Complete silence in meditation is the most effective in putting us in contact with Christ consciousness. This is what David is telling us in the bible verse Psalm 46:10- "Be still and know that I am God." Rev. Steve Clevenger, spiritualist minister in Columbus, Ohio, expressed the same idea when he said that the first step on a path of spiritual unfoldment is to become a daily meditator. This allows you to put God in control.

In closing this blog, I cannot over-emphasize the value of meditating regularly. Meditating in the silence helps us to grow spiritually. Spiritual growth helps us to progress in evolution. Advancement in evolution transforms us from human beings back into full awareness that we are spirit beings. At this point, we can live in higher dimensions called by some, HEAVEN.

Statements to Ponder:

1. God's Will will be done.

2. God dwells in me.

3. I AM the hands of God on Earth.

4. I AM here to do God's Will.

Blog 11

Does God Punish Us?

Yesterday, one of my sisters said to me that the COVID-19 pandemic is God's punishment of Earth's humanity for not doing his Will. I told her that God does not punish us. In fact, God does not meddle in the affairs of human beings. I believe that mankind is creating the world that we live in by our thoughts, feelings, and actions. We are co-creators with God. Because we are still asleep in consciousness, many of us are not aware that the higher, divine energies of God dwell within us. We have not awakened, or as the Buddhists would explain it, we are not yet enlightened. Because we are in this non-awakened state, we do not accept responsibility for our actions. It is, therefore, easy for us to appoint God as the cause of the consequences that result from our thoughts, feelings, and actions.

The way I see it, God is innocent of all of our misfortunes. He is a silent observer who watches over us and hopes that His divine energies in us begin to quicken strongly and awaken us to who and what we really are. Once awakened, we will choose to create in a manner that is compatible with the Divine Plan, which is the Will of God. Once awakened, we will stop causing harm to our planet and to each other. By choosing to make the world better for all, the consequences that we identify as God's punishment will cease. Please, don't blame God! May we all wake up soon!

Statements to Ponder:

1. "Whatever is spoken in darkness shall be heard in the light." (Luke 12:2-3)

2. "For you are all sons of light and sons of the day; we are not of the night or of darkness." (1 Thessalonians 5:5)

3. "Resist not evil." (Matthew 5:39)

Blog 12

Rebellion / Insurrection

On January 6, 2021, a group of thousands of insurrectionists stormed the United States Capitol with the intention of stopping our congressional representatives from certifying Joe Biden as the newly elected president of our country. This gathering was incited by the outgoing president, who refused to accept the well-documented fact that he lost the election. The coup d'etat was not successful, but now the country is very divided.

The outgoing president and a few of his power seeking partisan friends spread throughout the country the lie that the election was rigged. They had no evidence to support this claim, and it was rejected more than sixty times by various courts, including twice by the nation's Supreme Court. Yet, many Republicans in the United States still believe that the election was flawed and that President Joe Biden was not elected legally.

President Biden wants to unite the country, but many people believe that the partisanship is too steep, and unity is impossible "What is the solution?", they ask. "How do we move forward as a country?"

Firstly, I advise you to stay centered and be calm. Do not dive in and strike back, but as the bible tells you in Matthews 5:59, "Resist not Evil." Just be centered, pray, meditate, and let your light shine. The light will lift the darkness and eventually all will be light. All will be well.

In other words, the solution to our disunity is a spiritual one. When we grow spiritually, we shed our dense physical bodies and become light (energy) beings. The lighter we become, the more we realize that we are all creations from the same source energy, which some call God, the creator. God made us all. We are one family. We are all interconnected. The separation will disappear and one day we will realize that we are united. All problems that we are experiencing on the third dimensional plane will cease to be. This will be better understood when we learn more about the evolution of consciousness which I call spiritual growth. My book, Spirit Answers, explains in a simple, easy to read and understandable manner, how we grow spiritually, and how spiritual growth is the solution to the problem of disunity and all other problems that confront mankind.

Statements to Ponder:

1. "The Lord giveth wisdom: out of his mouth cometh knowledge and understanding." (Proverbs 2:6)

2. "A wise man will hear, and will increase learning." (Proverbs 1:5)

3. "Wisdom is the principal thing. Therefore, get wisdom; and with all thy getting get understanding." (Proverbs 4:7)

4. "How much better is it to get wisdom than gold! And to get understanding rather to be chosen than silver!" (Proverbs 16:16)

Blog 13

HOW DO YOU KNOW?

Last night, I had an interesting dream in which I was talking to the congregation of a traditional church. I was telling them that aside from environmental and sensory input, humans have two levels of knowing and understanding. The first level resides in the lower mental plane. At that level, we learn and understand by reading books, listening to teachers, preachers, parents, elders, and other mentors. As a result, we come to know and believe what they impart to us. This is how the majority of people in the western world learn. We learn what other humans teach us.

However, this level of knowing and understanding is not the creator's goal for earth's humanity. The most immediate goal is for us to grow spiritually and reach the level of the higher mental plane. After reaching this level, evolution will take us to the level of the buddhic plane, where spirit feeds us all that we need to know.

On the buddhic plane, like magic, we just know. Some call it intuition or gut feelings. It could also be understood as wisdom that originates from God, or from beings who have evolved to higher levels of existence. In any case, the information just comes to us. We know without reading or being taught.

This being so, in my opinion, humanity's energies would be well served if we focused on growing spiritually. By doing so, eventually we will not need books, preachers, or teachers to provide us with knowledge and understanding. We will have wisdom. We will just know..

Statements to Ponder:

1. "And ye shall know the truth, and the truth shall make you free." (John 8:32)

2. "Howbeit when he, the Spirit of truth, is come, he will guide you into all truth." (John 16:13)

3. I am the way, the truth, and the life." (John 14:6)

Blog 14

TRUTH

In my blog #13, *How Do You Know?*, I explained that there are different ways of learning and knowing, according to the level of spiritual development that one has reached. At the lower levels, in addition to environmental and sensory input, we learn by receiving and accepting what is offered by teachers, preachers, parents, elders, books, and other mentors. At the buddhic and higher levels, we just know. Information just comes to us. Obviously there must be energy/spirit involved in transmitting this "knowing" to us, but I am not yet at a point in evolution where I can explain this to you. I am, however, at a level to know that what we accept as truth changes according to our level of spiritual development.

Think about it. Much of what we accepted as true many years ago is no longer true to us today. We all now know that the earth is not flat. The teachings of Jesus, Buddha, and other spiritual leaders updated what humanity had accepted as truth in earlier times. As for me, my understanding of spirituality and what I now accept as truth have changed tremendously during this lifetime. This, I know, is due in large part to my spiritual growth. During the last thirty-five years, I have been consciously guided by spirit to people and activities that have helped me to raise my consciousness. This guidance is ongoing, and I welcome it.

The main point that I want to make in this blog is that we must be open to change. As we evolve, everything changes. What we hold dear as our truth today will be different when we reach higher levels in evolution.

Statements to Ponder:

1. "Verily, verily, I say unto thee, except a man be born again, he cannot see the kingdom of God." (John 3:3)

2. "Except a man be born of water and of the Spirit, he cannot enter into the kingdom of God. That which is born of the flesh is flesh: and that which is born of the Spirit is spirit." (John 3: 5-6)

Blog 15

YOU MUST BE BORN AGAIN

In my blog #14, I talked about what one holds as truth changing as one evolves. I also stated that everything changes as one grows spiritually. I did not specify that each individual human being changes during this evolutionary process. I believe that Jesus was speaking of this change when he told Nicodemus that in order to see the kingdom of God, a man must be born again. Nicodemus did not understand how one could be born again without re-entering the mother's womb and going through the process of birth again. Let me explain.

Humans, who are born of the flesh, change and become born of the Spirit. We change from human beings into spirit beings. Jesus demonstrated this to us with his resurrection and ascension. My book, Spirit Answers, explains the changes (called *initiations* in the Esoteric Philosophy) that take place in humans when they are being born again. It is a process of raising one's consciousness by transmuting dense energies into lighter ones. This process is the protracted evolutionary journey that eventually leads us back to the kingdom of God, otherwise known as the source from which we originated.

Statements to Ponder:

1. "Thou didst lay the foundation of the earth, and the heavens are the work of thy hands." (Psalms 102:25)

2. "The earth is the Lord's and the fulness thereof, the world and those who dwell therein." (Psalms 24:1)

3. "Have we not all one father? Hath not one God created us? (Malachi 2:10)

Blog 16

GLOBALIZATION

Webster's Dictionary explains *globalization* as: "The development of an increasingly integrated global economy." Personally, I do not think that globalization should be limited to the economy. I think that globalization should be the development of an increasingly integrated **global community.** We are all one. The divine source energy created all. This divine energy descended, created, and is all of us.

During the involution (descent) of source energy and the early stages of our evolution in consciousness, we lost our awareness of oneness. We became more and more egocentric. The individual rather than the group became all important. Now, as we progress in evolution, we are transmuting and raising our energies. We are becoming less dense and more light. As lighter beings, we are regaining awareness of our connection to everything. In reality, we are all interconnected. As I said before, we are all one.

In order for planet earth and all her inhabitants to be happy and healthy in every way, we must come together as one. We must realize that all countries and all people are one. All of us are creations from source energy, and we are all equal in God's eyes. No one was created to be superior to others. We were created to be different from others, in order to bring a diversity of entrees and main courses to the table. All resources should be available to everyone who needs them. No one should lack the essentials needed to live a healthy life. God loves and provides for all of us, and we should follow His example and do likewise for all mankind.

Statements to Ponder:

1. "Transmute, transmute by violet fire, all causes and cores not of God's desire…" (Violet Fire Mantra)

2. "God showed Noah the rainbow sign. It won't be water. The fire next time." (Charles Johnson's song: *It's Gona Rain*)

Blog 17

THE VIOLET FLAME

Have you heard of the violet flame? Many people have not. The website of the Spiritual Encyclopedia says that "the violet flame is one of the greatest little-known spiritual tools on the planet, and a tremendous gift from God to mankind." It is a violet color frequency of light which will be predominant during the two thousand year cycle of the Age of Aquarius which, by the way, has just begun. Of the seven major colors, violet has the highest frequency. It is the highest of all colors for healing.

So how does the violet flame bless us? It transmutes back into light our mis-creations from all times. In other words, it eliminates our "sins" from past lifetimes and from the present lifetime. The violet flame website says: "The violet flame is for those who yearn to break out of their negative family patterns, to free themselves and others from the ups and downs of human emotions, to heal wounds of the body, mind, and heart, and finally shake off the karmic chains of the past."

The violet flame will accelerate our awakening on planet earth. It will help us to shed our density and raise our consciousness. It will help us to make the shift into the fifth and higher dimensions more quickly. But in order to get these benefits, we must do our part. We must invoke the violet flame on a regular basis. As for me, I call it forth several times every day by asking it to transmute all causes and cores that are not a part of the divine plan.

In closing, I ask you to reflect on the lyrics of Charles Johnson in his song "It's Gona Rain". He says: "*God showed Noah the rainbow sign. It won't be water. The fire next time.*" Could this fire next time be the violet flame? Also, I ask that you reflect on the burning bush that Moses saw in Exodus 3:2. Could it not be consumed because it was a spiritual fire? Could it have been the violet flame? Maybe, maybe not. Some spiritual leaders think so.

Statements to Ponder:

1. In 2020, hate crimes against Asian Americans rose 150 percent.

2. Black Lives Matter.

3. All Lives Matter.

4. Thou shalt not kill. (Exodus 20:13)

Blog 18

RACISM

Racism has gone amuck here in the United States. I thought the fifties and sixties were bad when I was growing up in North Carolina. Then the Civil Rights Act was passed in 1964 and things seemed to get better. The overt racist acts became somewhat covert. This gave black Americans a feeling of acceptance and safety. So what has happened? Why are Black, Asian, and Latinx Americans now living in fear in the United States of America?

Many people would answer this by speaking the name of our country's forty-fifth president because he openly blamed and criticized people of color. He also excused and encouraged racist groups. During his four-year term in office, many lids that had hidden racist attitudes and actions were lifted and the world could see clearly the violence and unfair actions that were being inflicted on people of color. This is the state of our union today.

Because racism has surfaced and taken center stage in the United States, all eyes are focused on it. Many books and movies have racism as their major theme. The last three book discussion groups that I participated in chose to discuss books on racism in America. Practically every television and radio news program has a story on racist acts to report. People are being killed, wounded, and denied rights because of the color of their skin! Why?

In my opinion, white people are not superior to people of color. All people were created to be equal. Some white people think they are better than colored people due to ignorance, greed, and power. They have been taught to think this way by their ancestors. In regards to greed, it is a well known fact that for hundreds of years, white people enriched themselves off of the free labor that they exacted from black slaves. The blacks did the work and the whites got all the benefits. White slave owners exerted power over the slaves by beating and sometimes killing them.

Unfortunately, even today people of color are still being beaten, killed, and mistreated by whites for no just reason. The question is not: Does racism exist? It is: How do we rid our world of racism? The answer that I offer is: We must grow spiritually. Our consciousness will be lifted when we rid ourselves of the dense energies that are holding us down. We must transmute our mis-creations from this and previous lifetimes. Then, and only then, we will see clearly what we were created to be. Then we will all know that we are ONE, and we will act accordingly.

Statements to Ponder:

1. "Do unto others as you would have them do unto you." (Matthew 7:12)

2. "Speak evil of no man." (Titus 3:2)

3. "As we have therefore opportunity, let us do good unto all men…" (Galatians 6:10)

Blog 19

DO UNTO OTHERS

Let's face it! Hundreds or maybe thousands more years might pass before enough of Earth's humanity have advanced sufficiently in spiritual growth to rid our world of racism. This also applies to getting rid of the nonacceptance and mistreatment of people who are different from us in other ways such as religious practices and sexual orientation. So what do we do now, while waiting for us to reach this milestone in spiritual growth? The answer to this question is a no brainer. We simply treat others as we would like to be treated. We know what makes us feel good. Let's extend those actions and words to others so that they will feel good too.

Would you like it if people spoke evil of you? If they said hurtful things about you that were not true? Would you feel good if people criticized your physical appearance? Would you feel valued if people rejected the religion that you practice? Would you feel whole if others denied you the right to love as you need to? Do you think that you should be treated cruelly or killed because of the color of your skin? Should you be denied equality in education, housing, income, health care, and other necessities that give quality to one's life? I could continue with this litany, but I think you can see clearly the picture that I am painting. If all of us would treat everyone else as we would want to be treated, everyone would be better off. PLEASE let us all do unto others as we would have them do unto us.

Statements to Ponder:

1. "My God shall supply all your need according to his riches in glory by Christ Jesus." (Philippians 4:19)

2. "Therefore take no thought, saying, what shall we eat? or, what shall we drink? or, wherewithal shall we be clothed? …for your heavenly Father knoweth that ye have need of all these things. But seek ye first the kingdom of God, and his righteousness; and all these things shall be added unto you." (Matthew 6:31-33)

Blog 20

BEING RICH #1

What does it mean to be rich? To me, being well off means having all you need to live a comfortable life. We usually think of our needs in terms of physical assets such as food, shelter, clothing, transportation, healthcare, friends, and family. A middle-class family could easily believe that they are well off, and they would be right.

Being rich goes beyond living a comfortable life. Rich people have all that they need for survival plus much more. Many of them have multiple automobiles, multiple houses, expensive clothes, fine jewelry, huge savings accounts, and more. You might ask why some people have so much and others struggle to survive. Firstly, we must know that we come into physical bodies to experience different things and to learn from our experiences. Some people might have chosen to experience poverty or wealth in this lifetime in order to learn how people who are in these conditions feel, and how they deal with their situations.

Secondly, our holy books tell us that our Creator, God, supplies all of our needs, but first we must seek his kingdom. In other words, we must grow spiritually. We must purify our bodies and raise our energy frequency so that it matches the circulation of the energy of our infinitely abundant universe. When we reach this point in evolution, we put God (source energy) in control of our life, and our needs and wants come easily to us. Our needs will always be provided when our level of consciousness allows us to let go and let God.

Statements to Ponder:

1. "A man's life consisteth not in the abundance of the things which he possesseth." (Luke 12:15)

2. "Every man according as he purposeth in his heart, so let him give; not grudgingly, or of necessity: for God loveth a cheerful giver." (Corinthians 9:7)

3. "Give me your tired, your poor, your huddled masses yearning to breathe free." Emma Lazarus' sonnet – "New Colossus"

4. "He that hath mercy on the poor, happy is he." (Proverbs 14:21)

Blog 21

BEING RICH #2

We now know that when our individual energy frequency matches that of the higher divine energies, we can draw to us what we need or want. In other words, God provides. In some instances, people become rich by receiving properties and financial resources from parents and other family members. Others receive money from lotteries, or get exceptional prizes by winning high paying games. Quite often, those who obtain wealth by these alternative means, do not have the level of consciousness needed to use their resources appropriately. Many of them misuse it, or some even lose all of their fortune.

Well, you ask, what is the appropriate way to use one's wealth? Recently, while watching a reality show on television, I heard one of the rich characters say: "Life is about having." I gasped at the ignorance of the person who said that. Although she is a well educated medical doctor, obviously she does not realize that the quality of one's life does not consist of possessing an abundance of things. She also probably does not know, as stated in 1 Timothy 6:10, that "The love of money is the root of all evil". Having money and other riches is desirable, and some might say needed. Nevertheless, life is about more than being rich.

So, what is the appropriate way to use one's wealth? Firstly, I suggest that billionaires and multi-millionaires pay income taxes that are commensurate with their level of income. It was recently revealed that the richest Americans pay almost no income taxes. Our tax laws make it legal for these wealthy people to keep their money, while the rest of us support the country's needs by paying the percentages of our earnings that are required by our tax system. I must say that the richest Americans should know that although our income tax laws make their failure to pay sufficient taxes legal, this practice is not fair. I believe it should be changed.

Secondly, I suggest that rich people share their resources with people who are in need of assistance. As I said in an earlier blog, we are all one. I would not want a part of me to suffer from lack when I have the means to fulfill his/her needs. I believe that all religions and spiritual systems agree with me. Riches should be shared. Generosity is a virtue.

Statements to Ponder:

1. God is light, and in him is no darkness at all. (1 John 1:5)

2. Ye are the light of the world. (Matthew 5:14)

3. The Lord is my light and my salvation. (Psalm 27:1)

<u>Blog 22</u>

Lightworkers

There are many lightworkers in the world and I am one of them. I know I am a lightworker because I exhibit many traits that a lightworker is said to have. One such trait is that I have experienced spiritual awakening during this lifetime. I now know that I am a spirit-being like God, my creator. I have experienced being alive after leaving my physical (form) body. I have had visits with loved ones after they passed over. I have also had messages delivered to me by clairvoyance and clairaudience. Having had these and other spiritual experiences, I strive to improve myself by continuing to grow spiritually. I know that my purpose in this life is to achieve a higher level of consciousness and become a fifth dimensional spirit-being. I also know that I must help others to grow spiritually and improve their lives. These are also traits of lightworkers.

A lightworker is constantly bringing more light into his body system and into the world. This is a desired function for all humanity. Jesus demonstrated his light beingness in the account of the transfiguration that is told three times in the New Testament: chapters nine of Luke and Mark, and chapter 17 of Matthew. As one grows spiritually, one's body system becomes less and less dense, and more and more light. In other words, one becomes less of a human being, and more of a spirit-being because one sheds the heavy energies that he has accumulated by making choices that were not compatible with the light source energies from whence we were created. The end goal is to become, once again, a complete spirit-being. Lightworkers are farther along on this return journey than average humanity, but with the help of The New Group of World Servers, and participants in The Annual World Congress on Illumination, Soma Energetics, and other programs and events sponsored by lightworkers, all of Earth's human beings will eventually raise their energy frequencies to the fifth dimensional level and become complete spirit-beings.

If asked to define what lightworkers are, I would say that they are modern day prophets. Many of them are intuitive like the Old Testament prophets, plus they have taken on modern day tasks to lift the consciousness of average human beings. Lightworkers are a blessing to Earth's humanity.

Statements to Ponder:

1. We know that if our earthly house of this tabernacle were dissolved, we have a building of God, a house not made with hands, eternal in the heavens. (2 Corinthians 5:1)

2. There is a natural body, and there is a spiritual body. (1 Corinthians 15:44)

3 Flesh and blood cannot inherit the kingdom of God. (1 Corinthians 15:50)

4. A spirit hath not flesh and bones, as ye see me have. (Luke 24:39)

5. For he will give his angels charge of you to guard you in all your ways. (Psalms 91:11)

6. And he was in the wilderness forty days, tempted by Satan; and he was with the wild beasts; and the angels ministered to him. (Mark 1:13)

Blog 23

OTHER BEINGS

In Blog 22, I talked about Lightworkers. They are human beings who are members of the New Group of World Servers or NGWS. Lightworkers live on the lower consciousness levels of planet Earth (third and fourth dimensions). Like average humanity, they have not yet made the ascension into the fifth dimension. However, their energy frequencies are higher than those of average humanity. As you know, their mission is to help average humanity raise their energy frequencies so that eventually they will ascend to the fifth and higher dimensions.

There are many other beings who reside in dimensions that are higher than those where average humanity and Lightworkers reside. They are known by labels such as: Beings of Light, The Company of Heaven, Messengers of God,

Spirit Beings, Masters of Wisdom, Ascended Masters, Angels, Archangels, Spirit Guides, Devas, Extraterrestrials, etc. These beings are credited with assisting human beings as we strive to achieve the ascension by lifting our energy frequencies to the fifth dimension. The Extraterrestrials come to planet Earth from other planets. Some of them choose to return to their planet of origin after visiting with us Earthlings.

Many Lightworkers are aware that they have guides assisting them as they journey and help others to journey to the fifth dimension. These guides are beings who have incarnated on Earth as humans before. Now, they have ascended and are residing in higher dimensions where they have a broader view of reality when they serve as guides to Earth's human beings. They agree to guide us from the higher dimensions, and they know our purpose for incarnating on Earth. If we ask for their help, they will provide it if it helps us to fulfill our purpose.

Angels are also from higher dimensions, but they have never lived in human bodies. Therefore, they do not really understand what it is to be human. They bring to us messages from the creator, God. They also radiate light and love to heal our energy bodies.

It is wonderful to know that human beings who dwell in the third and fourth dimensions of planet Earth are not alone. We are being watched over by many other beings who dwell in the fifth and higher dimensions. These higher beings are more knowledgeable and better equipped than us. It is their pleasure to help us. Please do not forget to ask for their assistance.

Statements to Ponder:

1. God shall wipe away all tears from their eyes; and there shall be no more death, neither sorrow, nor crying, neither shall there be any more pain: for the former things are passed away. (Revelations 21:4)

2. There the wicked cease from troubling; and there the weary be at rest. (Job 3:17)

3. I will dwell in the house of the Lord forever. (Psalms 23:6)

Blog 24

THE FIFTH DIMENSION

In several blogs, I have stated that the next step in the evolution of consciousness for Earth's human beings is to ascend to the fifth dimension and become spirit beings. Planet Earth must also make this shift from the darkness of the third dimension into the spiritual light of the fifth dimension. In fact, in recent years our planet made this shift, and in order for Earth's human beings to continue to inhabit Planet Earth, we must also make this spiritual shift and ascend to the fifth dimension. This is our goal and our most urgent task.

How do we make this shift and ascend into the fifth dimension? We do so by raising our energy frequency. We enter the fifth dimension when our energy vibration is high enough to match the vibration of the fifth dimension. To raise our energy vibration, we must free ourselves of all the mental and emotional baggage that we have amassed during many lifetimes. We have allowed this heavy baggage to weigh us down and lessen our perspective of reality. When we release this baggage, our level of awareness becomes greater. The third dimension lower attributes are released and man operates from the heart. When the heart is opened and we operate from it, we are awakened to positive traits such as unconditional love, intuition, a mindset of abundance, and other spiritual gifts. When we reach the fifth dimension, we have a consciousness of love, peace, and compassion. At this higher level of consciousness, there is no heavy, negative baggage. Anger, separation, pain, sickness, death, lack, fear, violence, guilt, etc. do not exist in the fifth dimension. Life is totally blissful. Spiritual wisdom prevails!

Statements to Ponder:

1. All flesh shall perish together, and man shall turn again unto dust. (Job 34:15)

2. Then shall the dust return to the earth as it was; and the spirit shall return unto God who gave it. (Ecclesiastes 12:7)

3. God will redeem my soul from the power of the grave: for he shall receive me. (Psalms 49:15)

4. The Lord shall endure forever. (Psalms 9:7)

Blog 25

HEAVEN? THE END?

In the previous blog, I described the fifth dimension as a level of reality where there is no negative baggage. The dark, heavy energies that created our reality in the third dimension and the dim light energies of the fourth dimension have been released. There is no death, pain, war, violence, anger, fear, sickness, guilt, separation, or suffering of any kind. The fifth dimension is a reality of love, peace, compassion, abundance, and unity. It is all that is good. It sounds like heaven to me. If it is not heaven, it certainly is a step in the direction to reach heaven, because in the fifth dimension we are closer to returning completely to source energy, our creator.

The Bible verse John 14:20 says: "In my Father's house are many mansions." This, to me, is a description of the many dimensions that exist. Dimensions are levels of consciousness. Each dimension vibrates at a specific rate. Upon reaching the fifth dimension, we will continue to ascend into higher ones that vibrate at even higher levels than the preceding ones. Each dimension gives us more awareness and a greater perspective of reality. Manifestation becomes easier and quicker in the higher dimensions. We become smarter and all our needs are met. These higher dimensions, or mansions in the Father's house, could be endless. After all, the lyrics in the "Gloria Patri", a song that is often sung during worship services in Christian churches, say:

Glory to the Father and to the son and to the Holy Ghost,

As it was in the beginning, is now and ever shall be,

World without end. Amen. Amen.

Does this really mean that life is eternal? Could the "end times" mentioned in one hundred different Bible verses be the end of life for us only in the third dimension? After all, we now know that life continues in higher dimensions and we obtain the guidance of higher consciousnesses. Is the Apocalypse, as described in the biblical book Revelations, really the complete final destruction of the world? Is there really no end to God, the world, or to us? The answers to these questions will become clear to us as we continue the journey of raising our energy vibrations and reaching higher dimensions of consciousness. BON VOYAGE!

CLOSING REMARKS

I hope my blogs have given you a better understanding of who we are, why we are here, and where we are going. Before closing, I would like to make a few remarks.

Throughout these blogs, I have stressed that spiritual growth involves raising one's energy vibration. We can lift our consciousness and evolve from human beings to spirit beings by raising our energy vibration. Even if one is not striving to make the ascension, one can benefit greatly by raising one's vibration. By doing so, one becomes healthier, wiser, and more capable of attracting positive things into one's life.

I enjoin you to please consider raising your energy vibration. The Esoteric Philosophy states that one's energy can be raised by meditation, study, and service. Most religions embrace study and service, but meditation is not practiced by many in the western world. If you do not meditate regularly, I encourage you to do so. Mindfulness meditation, as practiced by the Buddhists and Hindus, is the most helpful meditation practice in raising one's vibration. Sitting in the silence, as the Quakers do, is also beneficial. Other practices that are very useful in raising one's vibration are yoga, invoking the violet flame, and exercises with sounds and colors. Soma Energetics is an excellent program for using sounds to raise one's vibration. Practicing forgiveness is advised by the Course in Miracles program, and the new thought religions stress keeping one's thoughts positive. All of these practices are helpful although it is said by some highly evolved spiritual leaders that quicker results are yielded by mindfulness meditation and invoking the violet flame.

Lastly, I encourage you to let your heart be your guide. Let love be the motivating factor in all that you do. Raising one's energy vibration opens one's heart. When your heart is open and radiating love, the world becomes better because you will make choices and act in a righteous, divine manner. When your thoughts and actions are coming from a higher consciousness, things change. The issues that we are dealing with today will all be resolved when we make better choices. Our government, education system, healthcare system, economy, and living conditions will all change for the better. The record setting climate issues that are now plaguing us will lose their destructive powers, and the apocalyptic scenes that we are presently witnessing will cease to be. Racism, homophobia, and other issues that strip human beings of their dignity will disappear. It is clear to me that spiritual growth is the answer to all our woes.

In closing, I ask that your I AM PRESENCE, which is your Individualized God Self, also called your Monad, your Highest Self, or the God in you, create an open, clean heart in you.

Much, much love,
Jacqueline M. Watts

GLIMPSES

OF A

LIFE

Jacqueline McNeil Watts

Acknowledgments

I owe much gratitude to the following persons, because without their teaching, encouragement, and support, this book would not exist:

- My partner, Dr. Marcia S. Howden – Thank you for editing the manuscript, and for the numerous suggestions that you offered to improve the quality of this book.

- My spiritual mentors past and present: The late Rev. Grace, Rev. Steve Clevenger, Rev. Dr. Catherine Clarke, Dr. William Meader, Rev. Molly Cameron, Rev. Rebecca Nagy, and Rose Ewald. Many thanks to Rev. David Hulse and the HeartLight Spiritual Center for powerful messages and love that radiates and opens hearts. Special thanks to Patricia Diane Cota-Robles, founder of *Era of Peace*, for the many opportunities that she and her organization provide for spiritual understanding and growth to all mankind.

- My esoteric astrologer, Susan Reynolds, who continues to impress upon me that I must share what I have learned with others.

- My angels and spirit guides, who never fail to provide assistance when their help is requested.

- To Infinite Intelligence, Creator of all – THANK YOU!

Preface

I believe that the writing, publication, and distribution of this book is the fulfillment of my preordained mission for this life embodiment. I believe so for several reasons. Firstly, the mystical phenomena that I have experienced during this lifetime prompted me to study and seek understanding. By doing so, I received the information that I have been urged to share. Secondly, I received (from higher sources), the idea and title for this book over a decade ago. Due to the busyness of my life, I procrastinated in writing it. Lastly, I was reminded numerous times during esoteric astrological readings and in dreams, that I must share what I have learned with Earth's human beings who are ready and open to examining that which I offer. Since you are now reading this preface, I assume that you fall into this category.

At this time, it gives me great pleasure to present to you: Glimpses of a Life.

Jacqueline McNeil Watts

TABLE OF CONTENTS

GLIMPSES

OF A

LIFE

"There is, in reality, only one lifetime that has the appearance of successive chapters."

David R. Hawkins, M.D., Ph.D.,
The Eye of the I, (2001) -Chapter 4,
p. 98

"By sharing this manuscript, I welcome you to bits and pieces of one lifetime."

Jacqueline McNeil Watts

CHAPTER ONE
(100,000 years ago)

Female A turned over slowly on her bed of grass-covered rocks and lazily opened her eyes. She raised her two claw-like hands and rubbed her eyelids, brushing the sandy particles away from her hairy face. As she lowered her right hand, it gently touched the black mole which was a permanent fixture on her face. The mole was just beside her right ear. Peering through the opening of the huge cave that she and her community used to shelter them during the night, Female A saw the light of the sun as it rose on the eastern horizon. It would be a good day for outdoor activities. Since she spent the majority of her life outdoors, her heart radiated a blissful hue when weather conditions enhanced activities in nature.

As she stirred and balanced herself on her two hind legs, Female A tuned in to the presence of others nearby. Three toddlers, who shared the sleeping space with her, were still fast asleep. In a far corner of the cave, a female who resembled Female A was quietly holding a baby close to herself as it sucked milk from her nipples. The female hummed a soothing tune to the infant. The humming, coupled with the alternate rhythmic sucking of the nipples and the soothing soft snores of the sleeping toddlers, created a harmonious vibration of energy that circulated throughout the cave. All was well.

Female A stepped out into the crisp morning air. Being accident prone, she took short measured steps. She wrinkled her nose in and out to inhale and exhale more deeply. She felt at one with creation. Yet, she sensed that something was missing. Not knowing what this missing piece was, nor how to retrieve it, she settled for focusing on satisfying her hunger pangs.

The others in her community had been up and about since daybreak. Several of them were splashing water on themselves and on each other as they scampered around in a spring of clear water. A bit farther upstream, Male A, the strongest and only remaining adult male in the community, cupped his hands together to scoop up and drink the cool pure liquid as it flowed from the crevices of a huge boulder. No one understood how or why the water flowed continuously from the opening in the rock down to the tranquil pool-like area. It just did, and by doing so, it made their lives complete. That flow of water was a vital part of their well-being. There was no need to explain it, it just was. Female A hoped that when the time would come for her small community to move to another location as they are often required to do when their food supply becomes scarce, they would find a new location with an adequate spring of pure, clear water like this one.

Female A walked around in the wooded area which surrounded the cave. She stopped whenever she saw something that she could eat. The woods were loaded with berries, roots, nuts, and leafy plants. Bird eggs were also available. Female A surveyed the provisions and chose what she would eat. After eating her fill, she broke off several large leaves from a bush and filled them with berries. Then she folded the leaves so that the berries would not fall out. When Female A had prepared a sufficient supply, she picked up all the berry filled leaves and headed back to the cave with breakfast for her young ones.

Every day was pretty much the same for Female A and her small community. Most of their waking hours were spent gathering food from their untamed natural surroundings and refreshing themselves in the tranquil spring of clear water that flowed nonstop from the giant boulder. Protecting themselves from danger was an ongoing requirement. All ears were opened wide, ready to hear the footsteps or the soar of wings of any approaching creature. If the energy vibrating from the uninvited newcomer was calm, all activity would continue in a harmonious manner. This seeming peace did not prevent the elders in the community from throwing suspicious glances at any newcomer for the duration of his stay in what Female A and her community considered to be their space. If the intruder's energy was agitated, as evidenced by movements in his aura, an attack was imminent. If the intruder was alone, defending the community was easy for it was all against one. If several intruders approached together, Female A's quiet community would have to declare war in order to protect their young and defend their space. Understandably, the outcome was unpredictable. Those who were the strongest, or who had access to the biggest stones and thickest branches always had an advantage. Having only one adult male in the community was a definite disadvantage. As combative as Female A was, her angry, combative attitude could not make up for the lack of fighting power that a strong male could offer.

Today started out like every other day. After feeding the toddlers, Female A took them out of the cave. The sun shone brightly and the fresh air was summoning them to partake of it. Being outside on a beautiful sunshiny day was an unchallenged winner to staying inside a dark cave where the air was somewhat stale and thick.

Once outside, the toddlers quickly spotted some children who were playing in the spring of clear water. As the toddlers headed in the direction of the spring, Female A instinctively sensed that she should go to the spring with them. Although the older two toddlers were steady on their two hind legs and had already learned to swim, the youngest was still developing strength in his legs. Female A turned to follow the toddlers to the spring when one of the females who was sitting on a rock outside the cave waved to get her attention. She stopped to greet the waving female. With gestures and sounds, the two females communicated for several minutes. Female A was learning of a tree located not too far away, from which she could pick a delicious juicy fruit that is just ripe. The kids would love the addition of this juicy substance to their diet. Female A was most grateful for this information because some how she understood that varying one's food intake helped one's body to function at an optimal level. By eating different foods, the body systems remained alert and active. If one's diet was always the same, one's body systems would become lazy due to habit and lack of change. The change of seasons was desirable in offering dietary changes to Female A and her community. Unfortunately, the only noticeable changes that Female A observed were from hot to hotter and dry to less dry and vice versa. Another possibility of a menu change was to wander farther away from the community's claimed space. Female A had just learned of a menu change that she could provide to her kids by walking a little farther than what was her usual food search trek.

Feeling uplifted by the prospects of offering a delicious new fruit to her young ones, Female A headed towards the spring of clear water. From a distance, she observed that the kids were having fun splashing each other with water and occasionally bending down to drink from the spring which measured roughly thirty inches at its deepest and less than ten inches at its most shallow level. Sometimes the kids would lie stretched out in the water, allowing it to cover their hairy little bodies completely. After a few seconds of being immersed under water, they would rise and resume participation in the splashing activities. What a refreshing way to pass time on a hot mid-morning!

On arriving at the spring of clear water, Female A smiled as a sunbeam shone on her face. She felt the joy of being alive.

All was well. She stretched open her right claw-like hand and positioned it like an awning over her forehead to shelter her eyes from the glare of the sun. As she did so, she consciously began to bring her toddlers into focus. She spotted the oldest one immediately. He was splashing water on a kid who was about twice his size. He was laughing as he lifted water in his cupped hands and launched it at his playmate. A few paces away, Female A spotted her second child who was taking a break from playing by sitting on the bank of the spring. After seeing the two oldest toddlers, Female A widened her view as she searched for her third child, her baby. She didn't see him standing in the spring nor resting on the bank. Where could he be?

Female A quickened her pace as she approached the spring of clear water. The closer she came to arriving at the source of water, the more anxious she became. She looked up and down both sides of the spring and did not see her youngest child. Her eyes scanned the bushes and trees that grew on the banks of the spring. Still, there was no sign of her baby. On arriving at the spring, Female A bent over and looked into the clear water. She saw a kid, stretched out, face down in the shallow water, but within seconds he hopped up. It was not her child. As she approached the deeper level of the spring, she saw a small body lying under the two feet deep clear water. The little body was very still. It felt stiff and did not move as she lifted it out of the water and laid it gently on the bank. Yes, it was her baby.

Chapter Two

(50,000 years ago)

The snow was falling faster and harder. The group of nearly fifteen human creatures huddled together to keep warm, which was practically impossible in these glacial weather conditions. Nobody understood how the nice, warm weather had become icy and bitterly cold so quickly. Fortunately, some one had had the idea of trapping and killing animals. The animal skins wrapped around them helped to stave off the cold. Plus, they were able to eat the flesh of the captured wild game. Plant life did not provide much in terms of nourishment during these blistery cold periods so humans were grateful whenever they were able to trap wild life, in particular bears and hyenas, which provided large skins for coats and large quantities of flesh for sustenance.

Male 1, who had separated himself from the group, was busy rubbing rocks together with hopes that their sparks would ignite the dry leaves and small twigs that he had positioned in the middle of the underground area. If the twigs were set ablaze, he could add larger branches and have enough heat to help keep his group from freezing. He had also learned that the flesh of wild game tasted better when allowed to roast in fire for a while. He learned this after accidentally dropping the thigh of a wild turkey in a fire. He retrieved it after a short while and ate it. From that time on, he preferred to put his meat in a fire before eating it. The others in his group eventually adopted this practice.

Fortunately, the supply of dried leaves, twigs, and branches was plentiful. Before the heavy snow arrived, all able bodies had helped to gather and store them on one side of the huge dark underground space. They had also gathered and stored nuts, roots, and tubular plants. When thirsty, they sucked on icicles and snow to keep their bodies hydrated. Surviving on a meager diet and in such harsh environmental conditions was a challenge that many succumbed to, especially newborns and toddlers. It wasn't hard to say that the lucky ones were those who did not stick around to face the struggles and hardships that accompanied human life in this time and place. Yet, survival was an instinctive desire in us, and we did everything possible to stay alive in our wretched environment.

When the fire in the middle of the underground space was blazing, Male 1 watched the smoke as it rose from the dancing flames and disappeared through the rocky ceiling of the space. Satisfied that the smoke was somehow disappearing from the area, Male 1 put a large, recently captured wild turkey on the rocks that had been set up in the fire area. Soon, the bird began to cook. The smell of the roasting meat, and the inviting heat of the fire beckoned the others to draw closer. They moved from where they were huddled and formed a circle around the fire. Male 1 signaled for Female 3 to come sit next to him. Female 3 timidly obeyed his request. At age twelve, she was the youngest of the three adult females in the community. The oldest, Female 1, was eighteen years old and she had already given birth to four babies, only one of whom lived beyond the age of one year. Female 3 had not yet given birth and she was fearful of doing so. She felt totally unprepared to have a baby, yet she knew that the day would come when she would do so.

Male 1 had a strong attraction to Female 3. He found her to be special and unique. Her smile was unlike that of any one else. When she smiled, her cheekbones and jaws puffed out like an inflated balloon. In the center of each puffed out jaw was a huge dimple. Although others did not find Female 3's smile to be particularly esthetic, it was the most beautiful smile in the world to Male 1. Her dimpled smile, coupled with a black mole which was positioned on her face next to her right ear, warmed him and made his insides tingle and feel full of joy. Whenever Male 1 looked at Female 3, a smile would spread across his face, revealing the gaps where several front teeth were missing from his mouth. When she would sit beside him, place her claw-like hand on his shoulder, or physically touch him in any way, he would feel like a firecracker that was lit and ready to explode. No one understood it, but yet it was obvious to everyone that Male 1 and Female 3 were a perfect fit for each other. They belonged together.

CHAPTER THREE
(20,000 Years Ago)

Dabi stared with great interest at the wall of the cave where his father had recently completed a series of drawings. The background was lined with horses, bison, and other large animals. Hunters with spears and bows and arrows in one hand and large feathered prey in the other hand were drawn in the foreground. Dabi wondered which hunter was supposed to represent his father. Then he saw it. The hunter with the black mole on his face, next to his right ear – that had to be him because his father, Toba, had a mole just like it. He also had nice dimples in his cheeks just like the man drawn on the wall of the cave. Toba prided himself on being the world's best hunter. He thought he could hunt down and catch anything he wanted to catch. Dabi had to admit to himself that Toba's hunting skills were very impressive.

Having located his father in the picture on the wall, Dabi turned his attention to the center of the room where his mother was making a necklace for the burial of a recently deceased member of their little tribe. She was also monitoring her daughter, Dabi's eight-year-old sister, who was putting on an animal skin coat that her mother had helped her sew together by using bone needles. The coat was a perfect fit for the child, and the deceased tribesman would be buried with a nice necklace along with several small weapons and tools that would make him well equipped to live a pleasant life after death.

Toba, who had been sitting quietly near the fire that he had made earlier to warm the room, stood up and, using a language unique to their tribe, told Dabi that it was time to gather food. Both Dabi and Toba put on buffalo skin coats and picked up sharp stone spears that were on the ground near the entrance of their cave. They slowly exited the cave in search of food. Hours later, as darkness was beginning to cover the land, Dabi returned home without food and without Toba. He came home to get other tribesmen to go with him to retrieve Toba from a wild beast that had attacked him. Dabi explained that he had run for safety when he and his father saw the beast, but Toba overestimated his strength and stayed to confront the animal. On hearing this news, Dabi's mother quietly began to gather materials to make another necklace.

CHAPTER FOUR
Nassor - 2450 BC)

Nassor gave water to two of his oxen and guided them to the pasture where they could graze with the other oxen and cattle. The grasses were thick at this time because the flood waters of the Nile River had recently receded. Conditions were perfect for growing crops and feeding animals. The river was the life blood of all life in this area, and it had provided an annual flooding as needed and as expected. Nassor knew that the gods were pleased.

The workday had been a good one. The ox-drawn plow had made the job of tilling the soil go quickly and effortlessly. Nassor was able to plant wheat and barley today. In a few days, he would plant lentils and other vegetables. His wife, Omorose, and their children, Pili and Shakir, would help. These crops, along with the fig trees, grape vines, cattle, sheep, goats, and chickens, would feed his family well. There would also be plenty to contribute to the storehouses of the Pharaoh, who ruled all of Egypt and demanded generosity from his subjects.

Being very ambitious, and loving to acquire stuff, Nassor did not limit himself to farming. Although his farming efforts produced enough for his family to live well, Nassor also worked as a scribe for the Pharaoh. This job was perfect for him for several reasons. During the dry seasons, when growing crops was not an option, Nassor wrote about Egypt in order to preserve its history for future generations. Nassor loved learning about the past and he wished that papyrus reed paper and vegetable gum ink had been available at an earlier time so that there would exist many more records of Egyptian history and culture for him to read. How boring life must have been before Egyptians invented hieroglyphics writing and paper and ink, Nassor thought.

On arriving at the courtyard of his mudbrick dwelling, Nassor was greeted by a dozen or so chickens that scurried away from the gate when he opened it to enter. The courtyard was surrounded by a high mud brick wall. On glancing about, Nassor saw two goats in the corner opposite the gate. They were being entertained by Sanura, the huge young cat who was treated as king of this mansion. Omorose, Nassor's wife, was sitting on a straw mat in another corner of the courtyard. She looked stunning in the linen tunic and straw sandals that she was wearing. Omorose was bent over a brazier on which pieces of lamb were cooking. Dinner today would be grilled lamb on pita bread with cucumbers and lettuce. Figs would be served for dessert.

After dinner, Omorose would have to meet her brother, and the two of them would begin preparing the body of a local resident for burial. Mummification was a skill that Omorose and her brother, Adofo, had learned from their father who owned the village funeral home. Deaths and burials were significant events for Egyptians because they had many gods and they believed in life after death. Omorose's local priest taught that when you die, the god, Anubis, would weigh your soul against a feather, and if your soul was heavier than the feather, which indicated bad deeds, you would be punished. If your soul was lighter than the feather, you would go to a new world and continue to live.

Other Egyptians throughout the land were told that the god, Osiris, ruler of the living and dead, judged the acts of men according to their merits. Many Egyptians regarded life in Egypt merely as a short preparation for the hereafter. The Valley of the Nile was a land seemingly devoted to the dead. The dwellers in this valley believed that the soul would eventually return to the body. Therefore, they preserved the body by mummifying it.

This evening, Omorose and Adofo would begin mummifying the body of their deceased villager. To do so, they would remove all internal organs except the heart and kidneys. Then, they would dry the body using special salts, wrap it in linen, and place it in a wood or stone coffin. The Egyptians built pyramids for the pharaohs and the members of the royal family. These great stone tombs were stocked with food, jewelry, and other objects that would be needed for afterlife. The commoners were not buried in pyramids. Nevertheless, they were buried with food and articles for their afterlife. Omorose and Adofo would have to collect the articles with which they would bury their village neighbor.

Spotting his wife cooking lamb in the courtyard, Nassor approached her. He bent down and planted a quick kiss on her cheek. Omorose slowed down his kiss by grabbing both sides of his face with her hands. When her left hand slowly rubbed his right cheek, she could feel the black mole that was located next to Nassor's right ear. When Omorose removed her hands from his face, Nassor smiled boldly, revealing deep dimples in his cheeks.

Chapter Five
(REBEKAH - 1260 B.C.)

"Palestine was a long way from the desert, which was the plain at the foot of Mount Sinai," Rebekah mused, as she laid in pain on what she believed to be her death bed. Rebekah knew that she was highly favored by Yahweh. To have lived for ninety-eight years without physical afflictions during such challenging times was a real blessing. As Rebekah continued to replay her life in her mind, she recalled her teenage years when her family lived in the Nile delta. Having been forced into slavery by the pharaoh, the whole family worked hard from dawn to dusk. Rebekah and her mother, Miriam, worked in the royal gardens. These gardens provided much food for the Egyptian people. (Rebekah had been told that her ancestors had migrated to Egypt from Canaan several centuries earlier because food was plentiful there and the Canaanites were experiencing famine conditions.) Being too young to be efficient at planting and harvesting crops, Rebekah's sisters, Leah and Sarah, spent their days gathering grapes, olives, and other fruit that was in season. They also helped to keep their camp grounds tidy. Asher, Rebekah's father, worked fifteen hours seven days a week, helping to build a majestic temple. Sometimes he would be assigned to work on other jobs that were equally as demanding. The work of slaves in Egypt was not to be envied.

Rebekah recalled how happy she was the day when all the Hebrew slaves left Egypt. "Moses, an eighty-year-old man, and his brother, Aaron, had finally persuaded the pharaoh to release us Israelites," she murmured. "We didn't have a clue as to where we were going, but we trusted Moses and followed him. There were hundreds, maybe thousands of us of all ages, genders, and sizes. What a crowd! Getting out of Egypt was not easy because the pharaoh changed his mind about freeing us and he sent his troops to capture us and bring us back to our camp ground. Moses' god, Yahweh, was definitely on our side. With his guidance, we were able to out-pace the pharaoh's soldiers and avoid being captured. We miraculously escaped the troops for good by crossing the Red Sea before it crested and drowned many of the pharaoh's soldiers, who were about to close in on us. That was quite an adventure! I just knew that we would be taken back to live out our lives in Egypt as slaves, but Moses, with Yahweh's help, kept us safe.

"After much traveling, and receiving food, pure water, and guidance from Yahweh, we finally reached the desert of the Sinai Peninsula. We lived in the desert for what seemed like forever, but it was actually about forty years. During this time, Yahweh continued to protect us. Many among us had not come to accept Yahweh as our only god and protector. We made offerings to idol gods. We also lived very loose lives. Poor Moses was not at all pleased with us. One day, he went to the top of Mount Sinai, leaving us to our wild, unruly behavior." Rebekah coughed, sat up, took a sip of water from the cup that was on a small table next to her bed, and rubbed her hand on the right side of her face, lightly touching a black mole located near her right ear. Then she laid back down and continued her reverie.

Let's see. She was recounting Moses' visit to the top of Mount Sinai. "Days Later, Moses descended the mountain carrying a stone tablet in each hand. Those tablets contained ten religious and moral laws that Moses' god, Yahweh, commanded that we follow. Moses called them: The Ten Commandments. These laws asked that we live as follows:

- To have no other gods before Yahweh;
- To make no graven images;
- To not take the name of Yahweh in vain;
- To work six days a week, and keep the seventh day holy;
- To honor our fathers and mothers;
- To not kill, steal, lie, or commit adultery.

"What a precious gift these commandments were! We Israelites gave up our other deities and agreed to worship only Yahweh, who was different from the other gods that we had worshipped because Yahweh had no human qualities. He was pure spirit, all-powerful, and present everywhere at all times. By following Yahweh's commandments, we came to realize that the main concern of religion was to guide us in discerning and doing that which is right and just. Our lives really changed for the better!

"A short while later, at age 120, Moses died. He did not make it with us to the land that Yahweh had promised, but we finally arrived there. Now I am back in my native land, Canaan, which has been renamed Palestine. I have out-lived all of my immediate family members. Leona, my neighbor and friend, takes care of me. I have had a good, long life." On saying this, Rebekah closed her eyes and smiled, revealing the beautiful deep dimples in each of her cheeks.

CHAPTER SIX
(RAM – 800 B.C.)

The sun was rising and Chaitanya suspected that today would be exceptionally hot. On such very hot days, it was best to get up early and get one's work done before the heat set in. Yet, she hesitated to awaken Ram, her fourteen-year-old son. He looked so peaceful and happy, she thought, as she stood beside his bed and looked down at him. His face was a medium-dark shade of brown, like most of the people in her Aryan village, who were mostly extended families, related either by blood or by marriage. Ram's eyebrows were bushy and his hair flowed down on the sides of his face almost covering a black mole next to his right ear. His puffy cheeks hid deep dimples that were a joy to look at when he smiled. Lost in her admiration of the beauty of her son's facial features, Chaitanya barely heard her husband, Nupur, call again for Ram to join him in prayer and study.

Nupur was a near fifty-year-old man who wore many hats. In addition to being Chaitanya's husband and Ram's father, he was the headman (leader) of his village and the local priest. He had inherited the priesthood from his father, and now he was preparing his son, Ram, to inherit it from him.

Being a priest was an honored profession in ancient India. It placed Nupur in the highest echelon of Aryan society. The Aryans thought that religious rituals were necessary to ensure plentiful harvest, domestic peace, and wartime victory. Since the priests conducted the rituals, they were highly respected and were given much power. Nupur was pleased that one day his son would become a priest.

The priests were also the main source for the teaching of sacred knowledge. In earlier times, they passed on this knowledge by word of mouth to certain people. This knowledge is now written down in Sanskrit in four books called the *Vedas,* and in additional books called *Upanishads.* Nupur is teaching Ram from these books. Ram would learn to recite the prose, poetry, and hymns contained in the vedic verses. He would have to pronounce each work correctly because it was believed that this led to prosperity and success in war.

By studying and reciting the *Vedas* and the *Upanishads,* Ram would learn that each person has an individual soul, and that all people, deities, animals, and things are part of a great universal spirit. He would also learn that when the body dies, the individual soul is reborn. Karma, which is the combined actions of a person during one lifetime, determines how the soul will be born in the next life. This cycle of birth and death repeats itself many times until the soul reaches a state of perfection. It then lives on as a spirit entity and death no longer takes place.

Ram would also learn from his studies of these sacred texts that love is very important. He would learn to love all, to be tolerant of differences, and to work for the unity of all people irrespective of religion. The Vedas and Upanishads texts were thought to be authorless. This means that they were not given to the Aryans by a man, but rather by an impersonal, superhuman being. Nupur thought that the teachings of these texts would one day be accepted as universal truths by all people.

Nupur stepped out of his wooden house and looked up to the skies. He felt the heat from the sun beam down on him. Wow! he thought. It was getting hot! It was past time to get to work. On walking back inside, he called to his wife: "Chaitanya! Wake Ram up! We've got work to do!"

CHAPTER SEVEN
(Li Qiang – 500 B.C.)

Festival time! The principality in eastern China near the royal residence in Loyang was preparing for a festival. The harvest was plentiful, the fabrication of silk was abundant, and the manufacturing of bronze weapons, armor, and other items was going at full speed. For these blessings, the leader of Li Qiang's principality, with permission of the king of the Chou Dynasty, proclaimed a festival of thanksgiving. The entire region was invited.

The festival would begin in the late afternoon when the hot temperatures were cooling down. It would continue until everybody went home. All the villagers were excited as they prepared for the festival. Various areas in the huge walled city were being sectioned off for specific activities to take place. A stand was being erected in the center of the market place for the opening service. All the villagers would be seated on mats on the ground in front of the stand. A rumor was being spread that a celebrity guest would participate in this opening service.

In a huge space near the center, where the crowd would assemble for the opening service, an outdoor kitchen was being set up. Many big fire pits were being loaded with wood and twigs for fuel. A dozen or more women, under the leadership of a well- known and very much appreciated village cook, Li Min, were busy preparing the food items that they would serve to the festival attendees. Barrels of wheat, barley, turnips, onions, soybeans, peaches, plums, melons, and persimmons were waiting to be prepped for inclusion in delicious menu items. There were also piles of chickens and ducks, and a large tub of pork pieces (mainly ham, shoulders, and pork chops) waiting to be dealt with.

In another area, board games were being set up. Chess and checkers were favorites among the residents of this principality. The competition was fierce and the prizes, donated by the leader of the principality, were generous offerings on his part.

Many of the artisans and metalsmiths had booths to display their bronze, pottery, and jade objects. Articles of clothing (silk for the upper class and hemp for the lower class) were also displayed. These objects could be purchased during the festival, or arrangements could be made to acquire them at a later time.

Last, but not least, an area was cordoned off for musicians and dancing. This is where most of the people would congregate after the opening service. The musicians made beautiful music with drums, bronze bells, and flutes. The villagers, young and old, would dance for hours without showing signs of fatigue.

The Opening Service

The crowd is seated in front of the stand, and the leader of the principality, Wang Wei, is addressing the crowd:

"Welcome ladies, gentlemen, boys, and girls," he says. "Our royal leader, king of the Chou Dynasty, who is our ruler by mandate from the god T'ien, is very pleased. You have done very well this season. There is plenty of food for our kingdom. Everybody will eat well. There are clothes for everyone. We have all that we need to live well and be happy. For these many blessings, we thank our gods." (The crowd cheers.) At this time, Wang Wei asked the village priest to come forward and offer a prayer of thanksgiving to the gods. After the prayer, the celebrity guest would be introduced. "Who could it be?" they all wondered. In a few minutes they would know.

"And now," says Wang Wei, "I am pleased to present to you our very special guest. Ladies and gentlemen, please welcome Master Confucius." The highly favored, revered teacher, editor, politician, and philosopher was here! Everybody stood and applauded when Master Confucius came from behind the stand and stepped up onto it. He began to share his wisdom with the village residents by offering and opening to discussion some of his well- known sayings:

- "Real knowledge is to know the extent of one's ignorance."
- "The more man meditates upon good thoughts, the better will be his world and the world at large."
- "Wherever you go, go with all your heart."
- "The strength of a nation derives from the integrity of the home."
- "I hear and I forget. I see and I remember. I do and I understand."
- "When anger arises, think of the consequences."
- "The superior man understands what is right; the inferior man understands what will sell."
- "Speak the truth, do not yield to anger; give, if thou art asked for little; by these three steps thou wilt go near the gods."

Li Qiang

Li Qiang was not seated in front of the stand, listening to the wisdom of Confucius with the other village residents. Instead, he was with his best buddy, Wang Yong. Both were in their early thirties and were married with children. They were both farmers. Although, like other farmers, they were having plentiful harvests, Li Qiang and Wang Yong were adventurous and a bit foolish. They decided to visit the metalsmith booths while everybody else was at the opening service, and help themselves to a few precious bronze objects. It was a crazy plan because their entire extended families would be blamed if they got caught stealing these objects. That's the way it was with Chinese families. The entire family was held responsible for the behavior of individuals. Knowing that he could bring shame on his family did not deter Li Qiang. He began to sort through the bronze objects and put some of the smaller objects in his sack. His buddy, Wang Yong, was doing the same. Then Li Qiang spotted a beautiful disk-shaped mirror of highly polished bronze. When he held the mirror to his face, he saw the black mole that was near his right ear. He smiled at his reflection and two deep dimples appeared in his cheeks. "Are you crazy man?" Wang Yong whispered. "Let's get out of here before someone comes!"

CHAPTER EIGHT
Alexios – 400 B.C.

"Moderation in all things" was a very important practice in all aspects of ancient Greek life. But when it came to preparing for the games at Olympia, perfection was the key word. Some would say that perfection was not possible without moderation.

Alexios, a twenty-two year old Athenian lad dreamed of perfection as he prepared for the Olympic Games which were to take place in a few months on Mount Olympia. These games were first held about 400 years earlier, and they had taken place every four years since that time. Boxing, wrestling, foot and chariot races, discus and javelin throwing, and free-for-all were the game categories offered. Only Greek citizens could participate. Foreigners could be spectators. Women were excluded altogether.

In ancient Greece, women were rarely seen out of the home. They were totally excluded from public life. Their lives were limited to obeying their husbands, raising the children, and running the household. Whereas wealthy women rarely left the home, poor ones ventured out to help support the family by working as dressmakers, wool-weavers, and midwives. Other than this work, the activities of all women took place at home. Therefore, Alexios knew that his mother, Agatha, and his sisters, Alexandra and Lysandra, would not be able to attend the Olympic Games and witness his victories.

As for his brothers, Erasmos was enamored with the plays of Aeschylus. He was hoping to attend a performance of "Prometheus Bound" at the recently built huge open-air theater. Erasmos had been waiting for years for this tragedy to be performed near his city-state. Now that it was coming soon, he had to choose between attending the play and watching his brother perform at the Olympics. It would be a difficult decision to make.

Alexios's younger brother, Kleon, was a student at The Academy, a school founded by the well-respected philosopher, Plato. Kleon was very bright and he loved learning about natural laws and how they governed the world. Kleon had every intention of getting to know himself by examining every aspect of his life, as advised years ago by Socrates, the philosopher who mentored Plato. Fortunately, Kleon's studies at The Academy would not prevent him from attending the Olympic Games. He would definitely be there to cheer his brother on to victory.

As Alexios approached the field where he practiced every day, he could see the Parthenon, a beautiful temple of white marble which was on the Acropolis, the highest point in Athens. "What a beautiful temple," Alexios thought. "The goddess Athena must be pleased to have this temple built in her honor. I wonder if the other gods and goddesses on Mt. Olympus are jealous," he murmured to himself. "Anyway, I will honor all the deities by my participation in the games. They will be pleased with my athletic abilities." These thoughts jolted Alexios back to the tasks at hand. He had to exercise his body and practice for his Olympic events.

Alexios would participate in the Olympics as a discus thrower and as a runner. He could out-run nearly all of the runners in his area, and therefore he felt assured that he could win at least one of the foot races. Winning the discus-throwing event would be challenging, but not impossible. Knowing this, he picked up a discus and began to practice throwing it.

Two Months Later

The Olympic Games had ended two days ago. Alexios won first place in the uphill foot race. He came in fifth place in the discus-throwing event. He was very pleased with his performances because he knew he had done his best. Now, he was participating in the winners' procession. Crowds of people lined the path where the procession would pass by. Alexios knew that his father would be in the crowd, trying to get a glimpse of his son, now an Olympic hero. To celebrate the victors, poems by the lyric poet, Pindar, were being sung. When the procession drew near him, Chares, proud father of Alexios, pushed his way to the front of the crowd and cast his eyes intently on the faces of the winners. He was relieved when his eyes saw the black mole near the right ear of his son. He smiled at Alexios. His son smiled back at him, showing off the deep dimples in his cheeks.

CHAPTER NINE
(Tiberius – 215 B.C.)

Tiberius laid quietly on his mat, which was a leaf-filled, cloth covered space on the ground in the fortified camp where he and his fellow legionaries had spent the night. He was not looking forward to the events of the day, so he procrastinated in getting up. His troop leader did not object to giving Tiberius freedom from the morning drills, since he knew that this young legionarie would soon cease to be in the Roman army.

As he cringed at the thought of getting up, Tiberius could hear his troop members. They were up, dressed, and going through rigorous drills nearby. Tiberius was drifting into a deep reflection as the members marched, putting distance between themselves and the camp ground. He knew that each legionarie was carrying a sixty- pound pack on his back as he marched, but this weight did not slow down the pace of troop movement. They had all mastered the art of marching while weighed down.

"Why is Rome always engaged in war?" Tiberius said angrily to himself. "It's one war after another. We have already conquered practically the whole world! Why do we need more land? Why won't General Hannibal and his Carthaginian troops stop attacking us? Why do all Roman men have to serve in the army for ten years? I am not cut out to fight! I don't like to fight, and I don't enjoy killing other people! I am so-o-o tired of these wars! I certainly won't miss them!" he said wearily.

He might not miss the Roman army and the fighting, but he would surely miss his family. When his family came to his mind, Tiberius smiled and the beautiful deep dimples in his cheeks appeared. His family was huge! His grandmother, his father and mother, his four sisters, his wife, Adela, and their three children, Brigida, Callista, and Marcus, all lived together. Also, three servants were a part of this household. Fortunately, Tiberius's family was wealthy and did not need the meager salary of a legionarie to live well. Like most patrician families, the oldest male was the head of the household. He had the power of life or death over all its members. He taught his children to value hard work, and to be loyal courageous, and disciplined. Tiberius sighed as he said jokingly: "Three out of four is not bad." Obviously, he had not learned the courageous lesson well. He knew that Adela and his three little children would hang their heads in shame when they heard about his lack of courage. How disappointed they would be. But not nearly as disappointed as he was in himself for bringing shame on his family.

Tiberius heard the footsteps of his fellow *legionaries* as they marched back to the camp site. Time was up for him. He put on a brave face when the troop leader approached him and said: "Get up and follow me." The leader led Tiberius to an open space which was encircled by all the *legionaries.* The leader motioned for Tiberius to stand in the center of the circle. Tiberius could not help but notice that each *legionarie* clutched a rather large stone in each hand. He shuddered and held his head up high. "Coward!" they shouted as they hurled the stones at him. Tiberius fell to the ground when a stone hit the mole on the right side of his face.

CHAPTER TEN
(Friar Antony – A.D.399)

Friar Antony was taking his early morning stroll in the gardens of the monastery. His task for today was to continue copying the writings about Christianity that had been provided by the gentlemen named Matthew, Mark, Luke, and John. Friar Antony sat down on a bench in the garden. He wondered what delightful information about Jesus he would read and copy today.

Smiling, showing off his big dimples, Friar Antony began to run through his mind the story of Jesus. He personally believed that Jesus came to earth to update Judaism, the religion of the Jews. Many Jews thought that Jesus was the messiah for whom they were waiting. Many others thought that Jesus was not the messiah and that he was attacking their beloved religion, Judaism.

"Both Judaism and Christianity are monotheistic," Friar Anthony said to himself. "We have come a long way from the earlier civilizations where many gods were worshipped. In addition, the Ten Commandments of Judaism offer an ethical code for living, which is very helpful and much needed by the Jews, and by everyone else for that matter. Both religions believe in life after death. So how does Christianity differ from Judaism?" he wondered.

The reflecting monk stopped his reverie long enough to swat at an insect that had landed on the big mole that was on his face near his right ear. The insect dodged the swat and flew away. Friar Antony continued: "Let's see," he said. "Jesus taught the beliefs of Judaism, but he modified and expanded on them. Instead of stressing the Ten Commandments, he reduced them to two: Love of God, and love of oneself and of others. Actually, the main message of Jesus is LOVE. He taught that God is loving and that we should put love above all else. This means that we must learn to forgive ourselves and others for all that we consider wrong doings. We must concentrate on helping others instead of on gaining wealth and fame for ourselves. By living this message of love, we will have eternal life, according to the teachings of Jesus." Friar Antony paused and took a deep breath.

He continued: "Unfortunately, many people did not like Jesus and they chose to not follow his teachings. The Roman government arrested and convicted him of treason. Jesus was put to death by crucifixion, which means that he was nailed to a big cross and left to die. He died quickly, but he did not stay dead. On the third day after his death, he arose from his grave and was seen by his twelve apostles and by some of his other followers. This convinced people that Jesus was indeed a divine being. Perhaps he was the messiah for whom the Jews were waiting. Messiah or not, Jesus's followers began to share with others what Jesus had taught them. These teachings became a religion that was named Christianity.

"Now, after nearly four hundred years, Christianity is the official religion of the Roman Empire and I, Friar Antony, am helping to spread the word by copying the teachings so that others may read them and learn. Good for me!" Friar Antony sighed. "Speaking of copying, I guess I'd better get to work." That said, Friar Antony stood up and began to stroll back to his work station in the monastery, where he knew he would spend the rest of the day.

CHAPTER ELEVEN
Sita and Jiddu – A.D. 500)

Newlyweds, Sita and Jiddu, were thrilled that their families had arranged for them to marry each other. Unlike many couples in arranged marriages, they actually enjoyed being together. Onlookers would say that they were in love. Sita and Jiddu's parents could see that they were perfect for each other. Well, almost perfect. There was one major issue that had to be resolved. Which religion would they follow?

In A.D. 500, there were two religions in India: Hinduism and Buddhism. The Vedic faith of the Aryans in the years 800 and 700 B.C. set forth ideas that were adopted by both of these religions. So which religion should they follow? How are they alike, and how do they differ?

Jiddu gently touched the right side of his wife's face on which could be seen a black mole and he led her lips to touch his. "Sweetheart," he said, "We must make a decision. Let's talk about Buddhism first. We know that it was founded by an Indian prince, Siddhartha Gautama, in about 400 B.C. The story of how this rich man ended up founding a religion is very interesting. Having lived a very sheltered life, Siddhartha was stunned when at age 29 he left his family's palace and saw much suffering in the world. He wanted to find out why so many people suffered from disease, death, old age, and other sorrowful situations. He began to study with Brahman priests and he learned much from them. However, Siddhartha got the answers he was seeking from meditating. These answers became the core of Buddhism, which was founded after Siddhartha shared with others what he had learned from meditating." "So what do we learn from Buddhism?" Sita asked her husband who seemed eager to share his understanding of this religion. Jiddu continued: "The main tenets, in my opinion, are (a.) Reincarnation, (b.) The Four Noble Truths, and (c.) The Eight-Fold Path. Reincarnation is the cycle of death and rebirth. In other words, death is not the end for us. After we die, we are born again in another body and we live another lifetime. This cycle continues until we achieve a state of bliss, called Nirvana. The Four Noble Truths explain how we achieve Nirvana. The first truth states that people will suffer until they are released from the cycle of death and rebirth. The second truth says that suffering is caused by people clinging to material things that have no lasting value. Truth three explains that if we become selfless, we can stop the cycle of suffering, and the fourth truth explains that selfishness is overcome by being moderate, otherwise stated as following The Middle Way. The Eight-Fold Path tells us that we follow The Middle Way by having right understanding, right purpose, right speech, right conduct, right means of livelihood, right effort, right awareness, and right meditation. So, my dear, that is basically what Buddhism teaches."

Sita replied: "Reincarnation sounds like The Law of Karma that is taught in Hinduism. One's behavior in the current lifetime influences his next lifetime. Good breeds more good, and bad breeds more bad. The goal is to behave in a good manner so that you can be released from the cycle of rebirth and achieve oneness with the great universal soul, or Brahman. It seems to me that Hinduism and Buddhism are very similar. Both religions teach that one must be released from the cycle of reincarnation in order to achieve a higher state of being. Although the Hindu worshippers believe in gods and goddesses, they believe that they are forms of Brahman, the universal soul. The Buddhists, however, do not worship a god. For them, meditation is the key. It takes the meditator on an inner journey to bliss. It seems to me that this bliss, or Nirvana, sought by Buddhists could be another name for the universal soul or Brahman sought by the Hindus." "That makes sense," said Jiddu. "So which religion will we follow?" Sita smiled, revealing deep dimples in her cheeks. Then she said: "eni meni mini mo…"

CHAPTER TWELVE
(Basima – A.D. 670)

Basima and Farah walked quickly so that they would arrive on time. It was their turn to pray in the mosque. Their two sister wives would remain at the homesite and pray facing Mecca with all of their children, who now totaled eighteen.

"Life has changed considerably in Medina since the prophet Muhammad introduced Islam to our people," Basima mused. "It's amazing how an uneducated orphan came to be the most important person in our town. Although he has been dead for nearly forty years, the impact that he has made will live on forever, and rightly so. After all, he was sent here by Allah to teach us and to lift us up. Muhammad's mother heard angelic voices when she was carrying him in her tummy, and the angel Gabriel appeared to him when he was praying and meditating alone on a mountain at age forty. After that first angelic appearance, Muhammad received many messages from Allah, and it was his duty to share them with us. He obeyed, as a good servant would. "

"Women are certainly much better off, thanks to Muhammed," injected Farah. "My grandfather had twenty-four wives. Now a man can have no more than four wives. Can you imagine having twenty-something sister wives? Having to share Hosni with the three of you is almost unbearable for me! Also, according to Allah, women are equal to men. In fact, all people are equal! Your race, color, gender, class, or culture does not make you more or less worthy as a human being than anyone else. Sometimes our men do not treat us women as equals, but we are equal to them in the sight of Allah. Now, we can even own property if our fathers or husbands leave it to us. Before, that was not a possibility."

"We have quite a few Jews and Christians living in Medina. Does Allah consider them as equal to us Muslims? After all, we are the ones who worship Allah," Basima asked with great curiosity. "Oh yes," responded Farah. "Allah loves and accepts us all. Allah is god to the Christians and the Jews as well as to us. They just use a different name for him. It doesn't matter if you call him Jehovah, Brahman, God, Creator, Infinite Intelligence, Source, and so forth. It's the same one and only God. The main difference between us and the Christians and Jews is that we know that each person can communicate directly with Allah through prayer and meditation. We do not need priests or holy men to make that connection for us. We are on our own. To us, Muhammad was a messenger, a servant of Allah. He was a prophet, not a divine being."

Basima stopped to tighten the scarf that covered her head. On doing so, her hand lightly brushed the black mole that was on her face, near her right ear. She said:

"I am so pleased that our family adheres to the major beliefs of Islam. We believe and have stated publicly that Allah is the one God and Muhammad is his prophet; we always pray five times a day, kneeling in the direction of Mecca; we fast from sunrise to sunset during the holy month of Ramadan; we give alms to the poor; and we will make at least one pilgrimage to Mecca during this lifetime. Hosni, Amani, and I have already made the pilgrimage. You, Malika, and our teenage sons will be the next ones to do so." "I'm so looking forward to that," replied Farah, her face beaming with delight.

Basima and Farah arrived at the mosque just as the crier was announcing that it was time to pray. They passed by the main prayer hall, the zulla, where the men were gathering. They entered a separate screened room which was designated as the prayer area for women. They each claimed one of the mats on the floor and stood over it and faced Mecca. Basima smiled and lifted her face upward showing her deep dimples to Allah. She then kneeled down on the mat and began to pray: *"In the name of God, the Merciful, the Compassionate. Praise be to God, the Lord of the worlds…"*

CHAPTER THIRTEEN
(Richard – A.D. 800)

Sixteen-year-old Richard turned over on his bed of fern fronds and moaned. He knew it would soon be time to get up and get to work. He could already hear his father, Charles, and his older brother, Philippe, stirring about in their family's cottage. It was a very humble abode made of wooden beams, mud, and straw. All of the cottages in their cluster were similar in size and in style. Unlike the habitations of the peasants, the lord of this European manor had a stone castle that was built on high grounds overlooking all of his properties.

"Our manor lord, Sir Franklin, is a very wealthy man," Richard said to himself. "He owns farming lands, grazing lands, forests, and peasants, also known as serfs. We peasants are obligated to serve Lord Sir Franklin for life. Yes, for life! In return, we are free to use the land that we work on as we wish. Our responsibility is to share with Sir Franklin everything that we produce, which is everything that one needs to live well. Sir Franklin and his family get their food, clothes, and all services ranging from carpentry, and blacksmithing, to midwifery from us. We do all the work, and they get all the benefits. Well, most of the benefits anyway. After all, Sir Franklin is responsible for protecting all of us who live in his manor from invaders."

Raising his hands to the ceiling, Richard whined: "Why, God, did you give so much to some, and so little to others? Christianity teaches that all people are equal. Yet, the rich have more power than the poor. Plus, the men's work of tending the main crops in the fields is given more value than the work of women who tend small gardens near the cottage, cook, make our clothes, and preserve food for the winter months when crops cannot be grown. The women work hard too! Why does our religion say that all people are equal when we are not? Is it because the holy book says that women are more easily tempted by evil than are men that we treat them as inferior to us?

"I hate to tell you, God, but things aren't right here. My heart aches to learn. Why can't I attend the school that Monk Alcuin just opened? I want so badly to learn and to teach others. I want to write documents that will help all people to live better. Why can't I do what my heart yearns to do? Why am I stuck on this manor doing farm work for all of my life?"

Richard paused, as if he expected God to answer him. Instead, his father, Charles, bent down and took Richard's face in his hands, lightly pressing on a black mole that was near Richard's right ear. "Get up, son!" he said. "Stop complaining! God already knows that you don't like being a farm hand. The porridge is ready. We must eat quickly and get to work in the fields." Richard smiled, showing the deep dimples in his cheek. "Okay, papa. I'm coming," he said. "As if I have a choice!"

CHAPTER FOURTEEN
(Mixcoatl – A.D. 900)

Mixcoatl sat on a mat in the open courtyard around which were grouped five flat- roofed houses in which his extended tribal family lived. This residential complex was located in Tollan, the capital city of what would later be known as central Mexico. Tollan was a large city filled with temples, palaces, ball courts, and colonnaded halls. Some of the buildings were made of gold. Others had accents of jade, turquoise, and quetzal feathers. There were also several large pyramids in Tollan with friezes on their walls. The friezes depicted scenes with jaguars, wolves, and coyotes: animals that symbolize war. They also had sculpted scenes of sacrifice such as rattlesnakes and skeletons intertwined, and eagles with hearts in their mouths.

Tollan was heavily populated by about 40,000 urban dwellers, the Toltecs. They were a warrior culture. Mixcoatl's family members were highly respected, very wealthy warriors. This was the reason why Mixcoatl was sitting on the mat. He was contemplating how he would live the next few years of his life. Would he go to war, or remain in Tollan with his loved ones?

"Let's see, what are my options?" Mixcoatl thought he was speaking aloud to himself, but his uncle Huemac overheard him as he stepped into the courtyard. "Options for what?" Huemac asked. "For my life," responded Mixcoatl. "Should I become a craftsman, a trader, an agriculturist, or a warrior? Our tribe has done very well in all of these areas, and I am strong and capable of doing well in any job area that I choose." "If you decide to grow crops, what kind will you grow?" Huemac asked. "I will probably concentrate on maize and cotton. They both trade very well. People really love the naturally colored red, yellow, green and blue cotton that we grow, and the maize is the primary food for both humans and animals. Both of these crops are sure winners," said Mixcoatl cheerfully. He paused to slap a fly that had landed on his face next to the big black mole that was near his right ear, and continued: "If I choose to be a craftsman, I will specialize in sculpting chocmools. All of our temples need these statues of reclining stone warriors. The vessels on the stomachs of the reclining warriors receive our sacrificial offerings for the gods. We must appease the gods, so we can never have too many chocmools." "Chocmools are fine, as long as I am not put in the vessel as the human sacrifice," Huemac said jokingly. He knew that respected, wealthy Toltec families were not usually chosen as human sacrifices. Unfortunately, many other people were not as lucky. "Seriously, I must make a decision before the tribe gathers tomorrow. I will be asked to announce my decision to everyone at the feast tomorrow evening," said Mixcoatl. "In that case, you probably need to seek the advice of your father," replied Huemac. "His counsel is always sound."

Later that evening

Mixcoatl chatted with his father, Ehecatl, who had spent many years of his life as a religious warrior. Although Ehecatl wanted his son to decide for himself how he would live his life, he offered guidance because his counsel was sought. "The gods must be worshipped far and wide," he said to Mixcoatl. "Other tribes must be conquered and convinced to worship our nature gods. We must appease Quetzalcoatl, our beloved feathered serpent, god of the morning and evening star, creator of the cosmos. We must not lose his favor. We must also worship and honor the lesser gods: Tezcatlipoca, god of war, night and darkness; Tlaloc, god of rain and vegetation; Centotl, god of corn; and Tonatiauh, the sun god. The gods are good to us, and in return, we must show gratitude and praise them. In my opinion, there is no greater way to honor the gods than to wage war and bring more worshippers to them. A man must do this while he is young. The other occupations can be practiced in later years."

The following evening

Mixcoatl's extended family was gathered in the open courtyard around which their five houses were grouped. Several members of neighboring family compounds were also present. A huge meal had been prepared so that the ninety or more attendees would all be well fed. The menu consisted of pulque (an alcohol beverage made from cactus), maize, beans, chili peppers, dog, turkey, deer, rabbits, small rodents, and birds. Everything was cooked to perfection over open fire pits. No one would leave this gathering hungry. But first, Mixcoatl had an announcement to make.

Everyone cheered wildly when Mixcoatl walked to the center of the courtyard wearing a headdress, chestplate, padded armor, and shield. He carried several short swords. "He's going to war! He will be a warrior!" they all shouted. Mixcoatl stood tall, encircled by his loved ones, and smiled proudly, showing off his deep dimples.

CHAPTER FIFTEEN
(Miriam – A.D. 1098)

Miriam ran her fingers through her hair. She tapped the black mole that was near her right ear and smiled, showing the deep dimples in her cheeks, as she looked into the beautiful gold plated mirror that her husband, Ruda, had given to her shortly before he left to fight in the Crusades. "Fight in the Crusades!" Miriam grumbled. "Why this stupid war? Why did the Christians declare war on the Muslims? What the heck was Pope Urban II thinking when be brought together thirty thousand soldiers (some of whom were women) from the Holy Roman Empire to take control of Jerusalem from the Arabs? What is so special about Jerusalem? So what if King Solomon's temple to God was built there, and Jesus was crucified and rose from the dead there, and Muhammad ascended into heaven from Jerusalem. If there is only one God, then why can't we all share this one Jerusalem? I don't get it! And I don't understand why the Christians and the Muslims are fighting to get more land and convert more people to their religions. Why do they need more land? Why does it matter which religion people observe if the one God is the main character in all of them? It doesn't matter if he is called by different names, he is still the one and only God who created all that is. I think these wars are about power and money more than about religion. It's a greed thing. This religion thing is so confusing to me! We all believe in one God. That one God created and loves us all. Our religions teach that we should all love one another. Yet, in the name of religion, we wage war; steal from, and kill one another. Will someone please explain to me how this can possibly be right, because it seems all wrong to me! This madness must stop!"

CHAPTER SIXTEEN
(Mansa Abdul – A.D. 1230)

Mansa Abdul wasn't wearing his deep dimpled smile today as he sat solemn faced on a floor mat in a dark corner of the large welcome room in his palace. He stared with a blank face at his throne which stood empty on a raised platform in the center of the room. He knew that he had to make a decision and he didn't know what to do. In the meantime, this young king who, on the unexpected death of his father, had inherited his position to rule over the Mandingo people in Mali, a great empire in West Africa, entertained what seemed to be a million thoughts that ran through his head. These many thoughts helped Mansa Abdul to avoid making the decision that he knew he had to make.

Abi, the youngest of the king's four wives, entered the spacious room and was approaching her weary looking husband. She was concerned about his solemn mood and thought that a bowl of hot tea might cheer him up. Mansa Abdul motioned for her to stop her approach, turn around, and exit the room. He did not want to be disturbed. Being a good Mandingo wife, Abi obeyed her husband and quickened her pace as she left the room. The forlorn king tapped rhythmically on a huge black mole on the right side of his face as he continued to entertain his thoughts.

"The Mali Empire is a young kingdom, yet it is rich and powerful," said Mansa Abdul aloud to himself. "My father was a great king. Thanks to his wise leadership, Timbuktu has become a busy and prosperous trading center. We trade huge amounts of gold, salt, and horses here. In the near future, we will increase the number of slaves that we sell. My people live well. We have plenty of food. Nobody goes without peanuts, maize, millet, and rice. We also have cattle and chickens, as well as the meat provided by the successful ventures of our great hunters. Yet, in the midst of all of this prosperity, I must condemn many of my people to death. How dreadful!"

The young king continued his monologue: "Why won't these tribes convert to Islam like my father did, and so many others have done? The majority of the Mandingos are now Muslims. We are an Islamic kingdom and we can no longer allow the savage pre-Islamic religious practices to continue. Allah is the one and only god. We cannot continue to acknowledge the many animal and nature deities that some of my people still worship. But, (he paused a few seconds) what if these other deities are real? What if they are all lesser gods who assist Allah? Now that's a thought that no one has addressed. Anyway, for the time being, I must proclaim that the Mali Empire is an Islamic kingdom. There must be no exceptions."

With a heavy heart, Mansa Abdul stood up and shook his arms and legs gently. He then went to his throne and gently slid onto it. He sighed heavily before picking up an iron rod with which he banged on a metal plate to call forth his warriors. "How will the griots recount this event?" he wondered. "Will it be a happy story, or a sad tale? Will my people believe that my decision was the right thing to do?"

Minutes later

Twelve warriors wearing breastplates and carrying shields and spears entered the room and approached Mansa Abdul, who was sitting quietly on his throne. They stood silently and looked attentively at their master's face while they waited for his orders. Mansa Abdul stared at his warriors as if he didn't know why they were standing in front of him. After procrastinating for what seemed like forever, with lips quivering, he gave his decision: "Kill them!" he said.

CHAPTER SEVENTEEN
(Linda – A.D. 1347)

Friar Micah moaned heavily and grumbled: "Hard times have definitely hit us here in Sicily. Seems that the whole town is dying. Dear God, what is going on? Priests, doctors, merchants, nobles, peasants, women, men, babies, everybody is dying. Nobody is exempt from this horror! What is this monster that we are calling the Bubonic Plague? Some people call it the Black Death because the swollen glands called buboes get big and turn black before the poor victim dies. But why is this happening? Why are so many people getting sick? Everything was fine here until a trade ship docked here a week or so ago. Did they bring this disease here in the goods that they unloaded? Is this a punishment from you, God? Are you punishing us for the sin in the world? Is this Hell on Earth? Will this Black Death end the world?"

A few hours later

Friar Micah arrived at the crafts shop of Thomas Ferino, a local well-known artisan. He had been asked to come and pray for healing for the much respected and beloved maker of wooden furniture, toys, and table-top sculptures. Friar Micah found Thomas lying on a mat in a corner in the back of his shop. Thomas was in great pain. Tears streamed from his eyes as he turned and yelped in response to the pain that he was experiencing. He had chosen to stay at his shop when the plague struck him so that his wife and children would not catch it from him. Unfortunately, his plan did not work. Thomas did not know, but earlier today, Friar Micah had been called to his house to pray for Thomas's son, Aaron who passed away shortly after the friar administered the last rites. There's no way to escape this dreaded plague!

Back at home

On returning home, Friar Micah ate a meager meal. He just was not hungry. Being around so much death had killed his appetite. Even if he were hungry, floods had in recent years swept through Europe and greatly reduced the food supply due to ruined crops and washed-away topsoil. "Our people are not strong enough to resist this disease," he muttered. "We are already suffering from lack of sufficient food. And now this! We are running short of burial grounds too. People have started putting the plague-stricken corpses together in pits outside the town walls. They don't want to be near these diseased bodies. Pray tell, Dear God, what can we do to stop the spread of death over our land? Has the Catholic church really failed the people here? That's what they are saying. Our people are giving up on Catholicism, and they are giving up on you, God. Please help us!"

The following day

Friar Micah is responding to another call to pray for healing. Senora Linda, the town's most revered teacher, has been stricken with the plague. When Friar Micah arrived at her house, her sister, Adele, explained that Linda had fallen ill two days ago. She was hoping that her sister just had a bad cold, but the fever, headache, and chills were followed by weakness and swollen bubbles (buboes). Adele put Linda to bed and washed her body with vinegar and rose water, as she had been advised to do. Afterwards, she cut open the bubbles, even the one that swallowed up the black mole near Linda's right ear. Lancing the huge bubbles would allow the disease to leave the body, she was told. Nevertheless, Linda showed no signs of getting better.

Adele led Friar Micah to the bed where Linda lay. Although pain ripped through her weakened body, Linda greeted him with a smile which showed off her beautiful deep dimples. "Thank you for coming," she said. "I am ready to return home to my Lord."

CHAPTER EIGHTEEN
(Nikolai – A.D. 1465)

The Plains

Nikolai, Egor, and Abram were busy loading wool and leather fabric onto the wagons to which they would hitch their horses. They would carry these fabrics to Moscow and sell them to clothing store merchants. These men had lived their entire lives as nomadic herders in a mild and fertile region of Russia. The grassland in these plains was ideal for grazing animals. Nikolai and his friends raised numerous cattle, goats, and sheep that supply food, clothes, and houses (tents) for their tribe. They always had a huge surplus which they sold to merchants in urban centers such as Moscow.

Not knowing how long the trip would take, Nikolai threw a collapsible felt tent in his wagon. He put a wool rug on top of the tent. The rug would make the ground a comfortable place on which to sleep. On seeing Nikolai include his tent and rug for sleeping, Egor and Abram did likewise. Although these herders spent most of their waking hours on horseback, they did dismount to sleep on the ground where they could stretch out their bodies and be comfortable.

Having finished loading their wagons, Nikolai and his traveling comrades paused to have a drink and a parting chat with the tribe members they were leaving behind to tend the animals and guard the camp. After downing a stiff, strong drink, they hitched their horses to their wagons, mounted onto the horses' backs, and began their journey.

Days later

Anatasia, Karina, and Natasha each sipped tea from their favorite mug as they huddled around the fireplace that was located in the back of their clothing store in the heart of Moscow. They welcomed this mid-morning break. Karina and Natasha were Anatasia and Borya's teenage daughters. Karina was fourteen and Natasha had just recently turned sixteen. Both girls were obedient, beautiful, and hard-working. Anatasia was pleased to have their assistance in the store that day, and the girls were delighted to have a break from their studies.

In the meanwhile, Anatasia's husband, Borya, and one of his merchant buddies were traveling to Toda, a farming community, to exchange goods. The round trip would take a full day. Winter was rapidly approaching and fruits and vegetables would become scarce in Moscow. Borya's covered wagon was full of articles made by his wife and daughters: hats, gloves, scarves, coats, and blankets all made of wool or leather. He was also carrying yards of wool and leather fabric that the women of Toda could purchase to make dresses, shirts, and pants of suitable sizes for their family members. On his return trip to Moscow, Borya's wagon would be loaded down with dried and jar preserved fruits and vegetables that had been prepared by the women of Toda. There would be enough to get Borya's family through the winter months.

Arrival in Moscow

Nikolai, Egor, and Abram arrived in Moscow after several days of journeying through the treeless plains of Russia. Their clothes were dirty and their bodies stank, but otherwise, they were fine.

They began their visit of Moscow by selling some of their goods to two clothing merchants. Afterwards, they went to a small family owned café for a bite to eat. Since their appetites were ravenous, they scoffed down pelmeni, stroganoff, salad, black bread, and black fudge. They finished by washing the meal down with a bottle of vodka. On leaving the café, they were a bit giddy. The alcohol was definitely having an effect. Nikolai sang loudly. He laughed, showing his huge deep dimples to all the passersby. Egor and Abram tried seemingly in vain to silence Nikolai, because they did not like the attention that the trio was getting. After what seemed like forever, Nikolai settled down a little. He and his herder comrades decided to visit another clothing store, since they still had a few wool and leather fabric pieces left to sell. They spotted a store a few yards away and walked slowly and unsteadily to it.

On entering the store, the herders were greeted by Anatasia and her daughters, Karina and Natasha. The men looked with lust filled eyes at the three females. They looked around the store to see if anyone else was there. "Are Egor and Abram thinking what I'm thinking?" Nikolai said to himself. "I believe we all have the same idea," he concluded.

In the blink of an eye, Egor quickly grabbed Karina and pushed her down on the floor, in front of the fireplace. Abram grabbed Natasha, pushed her against the wall, and began to tear her clothes off. Anatasia made a mad dash for the door, but Nikolai beat her to it. He locked the door and pulled Anatasia to the back of the room where he helped himself to her. For the next hour or so, the men took turns with the three women. Although the females fought and tried to scream, they were no match for the strong, flesh-hungry men.

When the men had had their fill, they motioned to the women to keep quiet as they opened the door and exited the store. Once outside, Nikolai felt blood running down the right side of his face. He touched the huge black mole that was near his right ear and realized that one of the females had scratched it hard enough to draw blood.

CHAPTER NINETEEN
(Griot Mame – A.D. 1560)

Expected Arrival of the Griot

Gao, capital city of the Songhai Empire in West Africa, was abuzz with the news that Griot Mame and her entourage were coming. People from the neighboring cities of Timbuktu, and Djenne were already beginning to arrive in Gao. They were claiming spots on the palace grounds on which to place the mats where they would sit and listen to the historical song of the famous traveling storyteller. Griot Mame was exceptional for three reasons: (1) She was the only female griot in the Songhai Empire; (2) She served the whole empire rather than being limited to serve only her tribal community; and (3) She was a trusted advisor to the emperor and other royal rulers. Griot Mame's visit was the most anticipated event of the year.

Hours later

The palace gounds were packed with an audience of thousands, all waiting with baited breath for the storytelling to begin. The heat created by the hot rays of the African sun did not bother the crowd, probably because they were accustomed to living in the humid, hot African weather. Griot Mame and her entourage of two lap drummers were sitting on a raised platform, directly in front of the royal palace. Emperor Askia Ishaq was seated on a cushioned mat directly in front of the raised platform. Rows and rows of Songhai citizens were seated behind him. The emperor raised his arm to signal that he was ready for the show to begin. Silence fell row by row on the crowd until only the buzzing of insects could be heard. The two drummers on the platform began to tap a well- rehearsed rhythm on the tin panels that laid across their laps. After listening to their rhythmic duet for several minutes, Griot Mame stood up slowly, pinched the huge black mole on the right side of her face, and began to sing her story.

Griot Mame's Song:

"Hello one and all," she sang in rhythm with the beat of the drums. "I'm delighted to be here in Gao once more, to tell you about this wonderful land that we call home." In a mezzo-soprano voice, Griot Mame continued to sing.

"We are the Songhai Empire, the third of three great empires that occupied this land. It all began hundreds of years ago when the Ghana Empire was created. This empire was rich with gold, and the Mandingo culture reigned. The king was looked upon as a god, the authority of all. The Mandingos expanded their land by capturing the territories of tribes nearby. By doing so, they also brought the religion of the captured people to Ghana. That religion was Islam. The king of Ghana ruled over the Muslims, but he and his people never converted to Islam. They held on to their Mandingo beliefs and worshipped a creator great spirit, and many lesser nature and ancestor deities. These Africans saw the world and everything in it as one interconnected whole."

Griot Mame stopped to draw a deep breath. She continued: "After several centuries of a glorious existence, the Ghana Empire was captured by Muslim invaders from northern Africa. This great empire gradually declined and declined, and it never regained its glory. It was succeeded in the 13th century by the Mali Empire, which expanded the territory of the Ghana Empire, and made Timbuktu its capital. Like the Ghana Empire, the Mali Empire was rich in gold and salt, and the Malians obtained much wealth by trading these two commodities. Unlike the Ghana Empire, the Mali rulers embraced Islam and made Mali the first Islamic empire south of the Sahara. All Malian subjects were encouraged to convert to Islam. Most of them did so. The Mali Empire was great, and like the Ghana Empire, it contributed much to the civilization of our world."

At this time, the tapping on the lap drums became louder and faster. The two drummers began to chant softly: "Songhai, Songhai, Songhai, Songhai." The audience joined in and gradually the beat of the drums and the word Songhai became louder and louder and louder. "Songhai Empire it is!" shouted Griot Mame as she smiled boldly, showing deep dimples in her cheeks.

The renown Griot Mame continued: "We are the Songhai Empire. We are the biggest, the most prosperous, the most educated, and the most cultured civilization of all times. We owe great thanks to King Askia the Great, who succeeded King Sonni Ali some seventy years ago. Askia the Great made our empire great, so we bestowed upon him the name: the Great. He had many schools and universities built so that our people could become educated. He expanded our land. We can now trade with merchants from Europe, Asia, and the Middle East. This great king was tolerant of other religions. The people he conquered admired him because he allowed them to practice their religion without persecution. We all know that Islam is the official religion of our Songhai Empire, and we live according to Sharia Law. Yet, our kingdom is peaceful and prosperous because King Askia the Great allowed others to practice their religion here. What a brilliant leader! Although he passed away some thirty years ago, we still enjoy the peace and prosperity that he brought to this empire, and I predict that we always will. AMEN, AMEN!" The crowd echoed back: "AMEN!"

CHAPTER TWENTY
(Christer – A.D. 1648)

October 24, 1648

Christer pinched the huge black mole that was on his face near his right ear. He was almost in a state of disbelief, as he spoke in a whispered voice to convince himself of the reality of this situation:

"Are we really here? Enok and myself, sitting at a table with delegates from various European States, Imperial States, and interest groups. This day has been long awaited. All of us who are present here in Osnabruck will review and sign the Treaty of Osnabruck, which is one of the main parts of the Peace of Westphalia. This Peace will officially end a war which has brought much discomfort to the world. Enok and I are delegates sent to represent Sweden, our country of birth. The Protestant powers seated with us are Denmark, The Netherlands, Holy Roman principalities, and our ally, France, which although Catholic, supported us to weaken Spain and the power of the Habsburg family. On the opposite side of the table are the Catholic powers: the Holy Roman Empire, which includes the Habsburg Dynasty, and their allies."

Christer stopped his self-directed monologue when the appointed leader stood and called the delegates to order. Christer smiled, revealing deep dimples that clearly showed that he was content to be in this room at this time. All the other delegates in attendance also smiled in anticipation of what this group was about to accomplish.

Several Months Later

Christer and his wife, Elise, were sitting at a table in the common area of their house. Christer was trying to explain to Elise what the Peace of Westphalia accomplished. "It brought peace to the world," he said. "After thirty years of war, we finally have peace. Much territory has been destroyed, many people have suffered greatly, and millions of people have died. And now, this conflict has ended and order can be restored in the world."

"Imagine," he continued. "A few decades ago, the Catholics and Protestants were fighting to determine which religion would be practiced in certain parts of the world. Actually, the war started as a conflict between Catholics and Protestants. Now, thanks to the Peace of Westphalia, Catholics and Protestants are defined as equal before the law, and Calvinism is also given legal recognition as an official Protestant religion. Each ruler now has the right to determine the religion of his own state. As for Christians who live in areas where their religion is not the officially established church, they are now guaranteed the right to practice their faith in private, and also in public during certain allotted hours. In other words, religious freedom has taken a giant step forward in our world.

"In addition to solving issues of religion, this Peace of Westphalia settles many other European issues such as the violation of borders and interference in the domestic affairs of other countries. Most important, it is showing us that peace can be established by diplomacy rather than by fighting and destruction. Thanks to the Peace of Westphalia, violence will cease, and the world will be a more peaceful place." "I will toast to that," Elise said as she lifted her coffee cup to click Christer's cup. "Long Live the Peace of Westphalia!"

CHAPTER TWENTY-ONE
(Veronique – A.D. 1750)

"Here I am, in the year 1750, married to Yves Chataine, and mother to Madeleine, Pierre, and Martine. All three of our children have left home and are living as adults. Madeleine is married to a struggling artist, Bernard, and the two of them live in a very modest apartment on Montmartre. In order to pay the rent and buy food, Madeleine writes articles for La Vie Quotidienne, a very young newspaper that is published daily. My son, Pierre, is studying at the Sorbonne. He plans to become a lawyer like his father, Yves. My baby, Martine, has not discovered what she is meant to do with her life. Presently, she shares an apartment with her best friend, Annette. To pay the rent, both young ladies work in a bakery in the university area. Yves and I are praying that she will decide to enroll and pursue a course of studies at the university. She has a good brain, and I know that she could easily excel in the academic subjects taught at the Sorbonne.

"As for me, Veronique, I am an educated housewife who spends her spare time writing pamphlets. This is a very exciting and progressive time for Europeans. It's as if the sky has opened and poured down fresh air on us. Men and women are beginning to become rational and think clearly. We are becoming enlightened about life and all that is. As Immanuel Kant suggested, our motto is: 'Dare to know! Have the courage to use your own intelligence!'

"My husband, Yves, meets regularly in coffee houses with his fellow male thinkers (we call them philosophes) to discuss and debate religion, slavery, war, politics, science, and the human condition in general. He tells me that the majority of the men who participate are strongly against many religious practices. They feel that traditional Christian beliefs restrict freedom of inquiry and thought, and that one should reject strict obedience to religious doctrine. Although they believe in an all-powerful being, God, who set the universe in motion, they reject organized religion. They are really repulsed by the decadent lifestyles of Church officials and by the practices of collecting exorbitant taxes and tithes from common people to fund excessive salaries for Church representatives.

"According to Yves, these discussions about how we should think and change our beliefs and our way of living are powerful. Unfortunately, most women are not allowed to participate. A few men, like the Marquis de Condorcet, believe that women are equal by nature to men, but most men believe that women lack the ability to make major intellectual contributions. To remedy this lack of participation, some of my educated female friends and I are holding meetings, that we call *"salons,"* in our homes.

"I am hosting a salon this evening. All the attendees were asked to read the Baron de Montesquieu's book The Spirit of Laws. We will discuss his ideas on the distribution of power among three branches of government, instead of having power concentrated in the hands of a single person or a single group of people. Montesquieu says: 'Government should be set up so that no man need be afraid of another.' He proposed that government consist of a Legislative Branch, that enacts the laws; an Executive Branch, that enforces the laws; and a Judicial Branch, that interprets the laws and punishes those who break the laws. This makes sense to me, especially since

King Louis XIV, a century ago, declared himself all powerful with his statement: 'L'Etat, c'est moi!' "

Veronique rubbed the medium-sized black mole on her face near her right ear. In a contemplative mood, she said: "I believe there should be checks and balances and separation of powers. I am anxious to hear what the other women think about this system of government proposed by Montesquieu." She smiled, revealing dimples in her cheeks, and added: " I just might make this the subject of the next pamphlet that I write and distribute."

CHAPTER TWENTY-TWO
(Rev. Joshua Wills – A.D. 1855)

Reflections on Abolition

Rev. Joshua Wills, a Congregationalist minister of British descent, sat in his favorite armchair in the parlor of his home in Toronto, Canada. He finished the coffee that he was drinking and he set the coffee cup down on the small end-table that was beside his chair. Rev. Wills rubbed the small black mole that was on his face, near his right ear. He smiled and the shallow dimples appeared in his cheeks. He was in a very uplifted space mentally. He leaned his head back against the chair and propped his feet on a foot stool that had been handily placed in front of his chair. He began to reflect on the past efforts to abolish slavery in the British Empire.

"They Desire a Better Country." What an appropriate motto for the Order of Canada, thought Rev. Wills. This motto truly applies to those who fight and pray for slavery to be abolished in the United States and in Canada. We abolitionists believe that slavery is an outrage against the laws of humanity and of God. We owe much to Upper Canada's first Lieutenant Governor, John Graves Simcoe, who was not afraid to speak out against slavery. Simcoe argued that Christian teaching opposed slavery. Furthermore, he insisted that the British Constitution did not allow it. But Simcoe's greatest accomplishment, thought Rev. Wills, was the legislation that his Executive Council passed, which repealed the Imperial Statute of 1790, and allowed settlers

to bring slaves into Upper Canada. By the repeal of this Statute, any slave entering Canada would automatically be free, and any child born to an existing slave mother would become free at the age of twenty-five. Although Simcoe's accomplishment did not rid the world of slavery, it was a great start. This is evidenced by the decline of slavery in Upper Canada and the three hundred slaves who were set free in Lower Canada in the early 1800s. Best of all, the British Imperial Act of 1833 abolished slavery throughout the British Empire. At that time, slavery was <u>legally</u> abolished in Canada!

Reflections Continue

Rev. Wills's thoughts skipped to 1851, when he had become a charter member of the Anti-Slavery Society of Canada. This Society was founded by the Honourable George Brown, who happened to own the newspaper, The Globe. This newspaper helped the Society tremendously by publishing anti-slavery speeches and announcements that were made in the Anti-Slavery Society's meetings. "Being a member of this Society is an honor," said Rev. Wills aloud to himself. "It has brought together abolitionists, both black and white, from churches, businesses, and the political arena, as well as representatives from the "Underground Railroad" refugee community. Imagine, serving in a Society with Frederick Douglass and Rev. Bishop Jermain Logeum! I am truly honored and blessed to be a part of this group."

The Rush to Canada

The Fugitive Slave Act, passed by the United States Congress in 1850, gave slave owners and their agents the legal right to pursue and arrest fugitive slaves anywhere in the United States. This law was abused tremendously, as bounty-hunters did not discriminate between free blacks and runaway slaves, and took them both to slavery in the South. To escape the risk of being taken by bounty-hunters, many blacks, free and fugitive slaves, rushed to Canada. From 1850 to the present time, the Black population of Canada has increased from forty thousand to over fifty thousand, and more blacks still arrive daily.

The Slaves Arrive

Rev. Wills was among the dozen or more members of the Anti-Slavery Society of Canada who were waiting for the arrival of the train from Buffalo, New York. This train stop would be significant because a group of thirty-eight fugitive slaves would arrive on it. Under the leadership of Harriett Tubman, they had escaped from Charleston, South Carolina, and were now arriving in Toronto, Canada. The trip had not been easy. As required by Harriett, each slave had made a pledge to die rather than return to slavery. They had traveled by night, through dark swamps, guided by the North Star, and hearing bloodhounds and slave owners in the distance. They had been hid, sheltered, and fed along the way by kind, brave white families who believed in the abolition of slavery so strongly that they chose to risk their own lives in order to participate in this slave-freeing effort. After weeks of hardship and worry, the weary runaway slaves were arriving, at last, in Canada.

The train pulled into the station slowly, and stopped. Harriett Tubman stepped out of a passenger car, along with two heavily muscled White male abolitionists. They walked alongside the train until they reached a freight car, and Harriett pointed it out to one of the railroad employees, who quickly opened the door. The fugitive slaves, who were hidden therein, stepped out onto the platform, tired, but extremely happy. They were in Canada! In unison, they kneeled down, kissed the ground, and thanked the good Lord that they were free!

CHAPTER TWENTY-THREE
Jackie and Joseph– A.D.2050

Joseph:

"Miss Jackie, at your very advanced age, you have out-lived everyone in your generation on both sides of your family tree. How do you explain this longevity? Is it coincidental, good luck, or just right living?"

Jackie:

"Joseph, since you are more advanced in evolution than me, and since you have been watching over and guiding me since the day I was born into this physical body in 1946, and maybe even before then, you know very well that my longevity during this lifetime is neither coincidental nor good luck. I would say that it is the result of spiritual growth, which has guided me in my choices and has prepared my physical body to benefit from the choices that I have made. As you know, I was not always on a path to longevity in this body. I must admit that my childhood was very sane and healthy. Although my family was large (I have six siblings) and we had limited resources, my siblings and I always had a roof over our heads, a healthy diet, adequate exercise, and secular and religious education. We had love and support from our extended family as well as our church family.

"Although neither of my parents attended college, they strongly believed that a college degree was the key to lifting one's station in life. Therefore, education was always an important part of my life. I was an honor student from grade school through graduate school. I loved to learn about all things and I did well in almost all subjects, algebra being the exception.

"As for religious education, I practically grew up in Mount Carmel Baptist Church, which was right around the corner from our French Street residence. Sunday School every Sunday was a must. This is evidenced by the perfect Sunday School attendance awards that I received seven years in a row. I was also a regular attendee of Vacation Bible School and Baptist Training Union. I enjoyed reading the Bible and learning all that I was taught in my classes at Mount Carmel Baptist Church.

"As an adult, I was very active in United Methodist churches. When I moved to Ohio, a friend invited me to her United Methodist church, and since I didn't see much difference between the Baptist and the Methodist teachings, I became a Methodist. Nearly thirty years later, after my spiritual awakening, my unquenchable thirst to learn more led me to study Spiritualism, followed by New Thought, and finally, The Ageless Wisdom/Esoteric Philosophy.

"Enough of digressing. I mentioned that I was not always on a path to longevity. This is so-o-o true. From age eighteen to forty, I was a pack-a-day cigarette smoker. At about age twenty-five, I became a daily drinker of wine, a habit that I picked up while living in France, and at age twenty-nine, I was introduced to marijuana while teaching English as a second language in a French sponsored high school in Luang Prabang, Laos. For too many years, I used these substances to bring me comfort and relief as I struggled through the challenges of being over-worked, having two failed marriages, accepting my true sexual identity, and losing my precious parents to disease and death. I hated my life, and the thought of longevity could not have been farther from my mind!"

Joseph:

"Miss Jackie, please tell us how you overcame these challenges and got on the path to longevity."

Jackie:

"Well Joseph, as you know, I never considered myself as being on a path to longevity. I did not want to live a long life, I only wanted to be whole. This wholeness, and many other positive things came abundantly into my life when I awakened from a low place in consciousness and began to help myself to grow spiritually."

Joseph:

"How did you awaken, Miss Jackie?"

Jackie:

"It's a long story. One could say that after millions of years of growth and learning by living in and out of many physical bodies, the time was ripe for me to become aware of what life as a human being is all about. Knowing that my dear mother was to die soon, out of desperation I asked Spirit to please let me know that my mother would be all right after she passed over. Spirit answered me by sending waves of energy up and down through my body. This answer led me to the spiritual path that I have been on since 1985. The most important revelation was that I became aware that everything is energy/spirit, even me. With this revelation, I finally understood what holy books mean when they say that God is spirit, and man is made in the image of God. It is true. We are made of the same energy/spirit as God! I also became aware of, and developed communication with, my higher self, my soul. Also of much importance is that I came to the realization that seeing burning bushes, hearing celestial voices, having visitations from angels and deceased loved ones, performing energy healings, and other phenomena that are reported in holy books is not limited to special people. These occurrences can happen to all humans when we awaken to higher dimensions by developing spiritually. With this understanding and heightened awareness, through increased meditation, study, and service, I grew more spiritually and became more aware of who I really am, and how I fit into this world. This journey has been incredible, and the amazing thing is that it is ongoing; it never ends."

Joseph:

"What does it mean that 'the time was ripe'?"

Jackie:

"To truly understand spiritual growth, I will refer the readers to my book, Spirit Answers. It is a primer which gives a very simple, easy to understand explanation of spiritual development. Although spiritual growth is a very complicated subject, my little book does a credible job of introducing beginners to this concept. The process of developing spiritually is protracted. It has taken millions of years to reach the phase of the spiritual journey that we are on now. Fortunately, at this time of accelerated evolution, due to the presence of the violet flame energy in this Age of Aquarius, humanity is poised to make a giant leap in spiritual growth. For me, that leap began in 1985."

Joseph:

"Did your negative habits slow down your spiritual growth, Miss Jackie?"

Jackie:

"When I awoke and began to understand who I really am, and I consciously got on the path to spiritual growth, I effortlessly began to release my negative habits. I can't take all the credit, though. I must acknowledge the help that I received from people like you, Joseph, who reside in the higher dimensions. There is so much help available to us from the higher planes. There are also lightworkers on this third-dimensional plane helping us. We just have to wake up and become aware of them."

Joseph:

"You mentioned the third-dimensional plane. Do you really think that you are still residing in the third-dimensional plane consciousness?"

Jackie:

"To be honest, I must say no. I was told by a very spiritually evolved lightworker that planet Earth shifted into the fifth dimension in 2012. I believe that my consciousness level has also shifted upward considerably since that time. I suspect that I am living much of the time in the fifth-dimensional plane now because my body is withstanding much higher rates of vibration than it could seventy-five years ago. Also, I can see light radiating from my body, just like it does from the physical sun. But as for humanity as a whole, I think that many of Earth's human beings are still residing in the consciousness level of the third and fourth dimensions, although they have taken the steps to enter the initial frequencies of the fifth-dimensional plane. This is why there are so many lightworkers offering assistance to help us lift ourselves into higher frequencies of the fifth dimension. I hope they succeed in helping everyone to make the shift, because the fifth-dimensional plane, The New Earth, will not be able to support beings of lower consciousness. Such humans will not be able to be reborn on planet Earth after this current lifetime unless they learn needed lessons and lift their consciousness by attending schools while in the inner planes. Otherwise, they will have to find a place with a lower vibratory rate on which to live." (This said, Miss Jackie rubbed the tiny black mole near her right ear and smiled, showing Joseph the shallow dimples in her cheeks.)

Joseph:

"I have confidence in Earth's humanity. I think they will all make it to The New Earth. After all, you humans have come a long way, and you haven't given up. It blows my mind when I think of all the religions, prophets, and messengers that have guided you during this evolutionary journey. They all have a purpose, and they all are fulfilling their purpose. They are helping you, in one way or another, to advance on your journey to the realization that you are spirit beings and are functioning as such. Each religion has its own way of interpreting and explaining, and each believes that its way is the best. In my opinion, no one is better than the others. I see them as useful because they will all play an important role in helping humanity to reach its destination. The difference lies in the amount of time that it will take to reach that destination. As for you human beings, your main challenge is to become aware of the role that you must play in order to move forward quickly on this spiritual journey. Religions have tried to teach and guide you, but the real work is the responsibility of each individual. Each one of you must do your part in order to make the shift from human being to spirit being. Your task is to lift your consciousness by growing spiritually. And as I said before, I have confidence in you. I think you will all make it to The New Earth."

CHAPTER TWENTY-FOUR
(Jackie – The Future, Exact Time Unknown)

"Well here I am, Jackie Watts, resident of The New Earth. My mole and dimples, as well as other physical body features, have disappeared, but mentally, I know that I am still me. I can't say what year it is because there is no time here in the fifth-dimensional plane. I don't know how long I have been here, nor how long I will be here. I only know that now, I am here.

"Some people say that The New Earth, the fifth-dimensional plane, is The Kingdom of Heaven that was taught in the traditional religions many years ago. It could very well be, but if so, I now know that there were some misconceptions about this place. It is simply a plane with a higher vibratory rate than we had when we lived in the third dimension. We became equipped to live in this plane of higher vibration when we raised our personal energy from the lower third dimension to the fourth and then the higher fifth dimension vibration. In other words, we lifted and perfected ourselves by growing spiritually. By doing so, we evolved from a 'human being' to a 'spirit being'. All of us who live on The New Earth are spirit beings. This was the next stage in evolution for Earth's humanity. This was what Jesus, through his resurrection and ascension, was demonstrating to us. Since we are now here, I can say that we have all reached that stage in evolution. Hooray!

"You are probably wondering what it means to be a spirit being. What is different? Most apparent are the changes that have taken place in our bodies. We have perfected ourselves. Every atom in our bodies has changed for the better. As human beings, we were carbon-based. Now we are crystalline-based. Look at how we glow! This change should not be difficult for us to understand. After all, over much time, coarse rocks can evolve into translucent crystals and sparking diamonds. This same evolutionary concept applies to us. Having raised our vibratory rate, we no longer appear to be solid, because we are not. We appear more like the energy/spirit beings that we are. We radiate light and we glow. All of our chakras (energy wheels) are operating at full speed. We know that we are receiving our power through energy radiations, and these radiations are our individualized flow of source energy that some of you refer to as God. Thus, we realize how we are all one with God. We respect this power source, and we obey its guidance. This makes our lives perfect here, on The New earth.

"Speaking of perfection, I say again that everything is perfect here on The New Earth. All of the old Earth's humanity had to transmute all negativity before we could ascend to this higher plane. The positive energy of love had to reign. In the fifth dimension, there is no discord, no illness, no aging, no war, no pain, no suffering, no poverty, no greed, no corruption, no lying, no cheating, no stealing, and best of all, no death. Since our dense bodies no longer exist, there is no sex and no childbirth. In this higher dimension, we know that we are all equal. There is no discrimination at all. No one is superior to anyone else in any way. There is nothing negative here! It is all good, positive energy. It is all LOVE. It is all LIGHT. It is all GOD. This New Earth is indeed heaven! And all of Earth's humanity is now living here in peace and harmony.

"Where do we go from here? I really don't know. I do know, however, that we will continue to exist because life is without end. Where, how, and why we will exist has not yet been revealed to me. I am convinced, however, that there is a Divine

Plan. Farther along, the next stage will be revealed to us. As for the time being, I don't know where the next phase of evolution will lead me, so I will relax and enjoy The New Earth where I am now. I am truly grateful!"

THE END

References

Farrington, Karen. The History of Religion. New York: Barnes & Noble, 2001.

Hawkins, David R., M.D., Ph.D., <u>The Eye of the I.</u> W. Sedona, Arizona: Veritas Publishing, 2001, Chapter 4, Page 98.

Stearns, Peter N., Donald R. Schwartz, and Barry K. Beyer. World History: Traditions and New Directions. Menlo Park, California: Addison-Wesley Publishing Company, Inc., 1991.

Van Loon, Hendrik Willem. The Story of Mankind. New York: H. Liveright Publishing, 1921.

The World Wide Web.

Spirit Answers

(A Primer to Understanding Spiritual Growth)

By Jacqueline McNeil Watts

TABLE OF CONTENTS

Preface

In 2001, I wrote a book for my family in which I described how my parents, with very meager resources and many obstacles, raised all seven of their children to become productive, college educated professionals. Since that book was about my family, I distributed it only to family members. It was never published.

In 2015, while on an outing with my great niece, Vyasia, she enthusiastically told me that her grandmother, who is my oldest sister, had shared my book with her. Vyasia thought the book was informative and helpful, and suggested that I continue to write.

A few months later, in February, 2016, an esoteric astrologer told me, during a reading of my chart, that I must share my writing to lift others. Ironically, while doing the chart reading, the astrologer did not know that I had ever written anything. She just saw in my chart that I came into this lifetime gifted to write, and led by spirit to help others. I would have blown off this reading if I had not received this very same message in the past from at least five other readers. One's natal chart does not change; nor does it lie.

Encouraged by the endorsements of my great niece and my current esoteric astrologer, I began to give birth to a new effort entitled Spirit Answers. This book is a primer to understanding spiritual growth. It gives a basic, very simplified explanation of what we are and of our evolution from human beings to spirit beings. The book is written in a question-answer format.

I ask Spirit for explanations and Spirit guides me in answering my queries. All lives in physical bodies are guided by Spirit, whether we are aware of it or not. Some people listen, hear, and comply while other ignore the spiritual guidance that they are given. **Both reactions lead to growth.**

Are you puzzled by the previous statement? Please read on.

Foreword

Times they are a-changin'. If you are of the "glass is half empty" persuasion then you will look around and see poverty, addiction, disease, sectarian violence, and other ills that beset humanity. But if you take the long view, you will realize that humanity has come a long way. Yes, we are waking up.

We are evolving, a never-ending process that brings us closer and closer to the qualities of the divinity that created us. If we take the time to compare our current situation to the situation of humanity even just a few centuries ago, we can see that people are beginning to realize the fundamental oneness of all creation. Suffrage is no longer limited to just a small segment of the population (e.g., white, male property owners). International foundations extend their efforts to take health care, decent housing, education, and nutrition to many of the world's most vulnerable citizens. And the environmental movement has shown us that we must be stewards of the earth: what hurts any part of creation hurts all of creation.

In her dialogue with Spirit, Jacqueline Watts sets forth an understanding of the all-encompassing divine energy that is our universe. She shows how this energy is both our current make-up and our destiny. Joining her on this evolutionary journey will be an unforgettable and rewarding experience.

Marcia S. Howden, Ph.D.

Acknowledgements

I would like to acknowledge the support received from the following entities because without them, the writing of this book would not have been possible:

- God and my spirit guidance – I honor you. I love you. I thank you.

- My parents, the late Samuel and Mary McNeil – Thank you for raising me with Christian values.

- My partner, Dr. Marcia Howden – Thank you for writing the foreword and for editing this book.

- Unity Institute in Lees Summit, Missouri, The Center for Spiritual Living in Columbus, Ohio, and The School for Esoteric Studies in Asheville, North Carolina – Thank you for clarifying my understanding of spirituality with the many courses that you provided.

- My spiritual mentors: The late Rev. Grace, Rev. Steve Clevenger, Rev. Dr. Catherine Clarke, William E. Meader, Rose Ewald, and Patricia Diane Cota-Robles – Thank you, thank you, thank you. Words cannot express my appreciation for all that I have learned from you.

- Rev. Rebecca Nagy – Thank you for creating the illustrations for this book and for being a dedicated spiritual leader.

Jacqueline McNeil Watts

April, 2016

DEDICATION

This book is dedicated to Spirit, for without your numerous promptings, I would not have taken on this project, and without your assistance, this book would not have been written.

This book is also dedicated to my great niece, Vyasia Johnson, and to my esoteric astrologer, Susan Reynolds. Thank you for encouraging me to write and to share my writing.

This book is further dedicated to everyone who reads it. May it bring clarity to your understanding of who you are and why you are here.

Lastly, this book is dedicated to all of Earth's humanity. May we accelerate our spiritual growth, and may we know and embrace all life as ONE.

If we live by the Spirit, by the Spirit let us also walk. (ASV)

Galatians 5:25

February 23, 2016

Dear Spirit,

We are beginning to write a book in which you will play a gigantic role. I will present situations and/or ask questions. I am counting on you to provide explanations and answers to my queries. To begin, it would be helpful for the readers to know who you are. When I write to Spirit, to whom am I addressing this question?

Blessings,

Jackie

February 24, 2016

Spirit Answers:

Only you can know for sure the Spirit that is responding to your queries. Spirit is all that is. God is spirit and humans are spirit beings having a human experience. Between God and humans there is nothing but spirit. Spirit is energy. Energies have varying qualities and degrees of potency. The energy that is God is all powerful. It is the source of all creation. The energy that is man is source energy that has been greatly diminished. In between God transcendent (Source) and physical man who dwells on planet Earth, there are many different levels of spirit. The level closest to man is his soul or higher self. Man's highest self is his personalized God or God immanent. Yes, God is both near and far. God is spirit, and spirit is all that is. *(Diagram 1 – The Three Parts of Man)*

I must not fail to mention the multitudes of spirit beings that reside on various planes of the universe. These range from souls that have been recently released from physical bodies through death, to angels, archangels, masters of wisdom, lords of the seven rays, and so on. These spirit entities possess varying levels of source (divine) energy. Therefore, their level of consciousness (awareness) of all that exists varies. Eventually, this path of energies ends at God, source energy, creator of all that is.

Jackie Replies:

All is spirit and all comes from the one source which we call God. My answers can be emanating from one of many levels of spirit beings. I am capitalizing Spirit when I refer to you, my assistant in writing this book, to make it clear that my answers are coming from a consciousness level that is more evolved than my personality self. The Spirit who is assisting me has more of the higher, refined, source energies than I have and is therefore more knowledgeable than I. I am grateful for his/her guidance.

Diagram 1 - The Three Parts of Man

MONAD: Highest Self

SOUL: Higher Self

Personality

February 25, 2016

Dear Spirit,

Some New Thought adherents refer to God as "Mother/ Father God" How can God be both mother and father?

Blessings,

Jackie

Spirit Answers:

God is spirit and spirit is energy. The great source energy that we call God breaks down into seven distinct energies that we call the seven rays. The first three rays are major and they comprise all of Source or God. The other four rays are offshoots of the third ray. All seven rays are potent and important. Each ray radiates qualities that are essential to the health and wholeness of all creation.

This great source energy, comprised of many qualities, is similar to the phenomenon of white light as it breaks down into its component parts when it passes through a prism. Each color is distinguished by its own frequency and characteristics. Together they make up the beauty, power, and complexity of the visible world. Likewise, each ray has its distinguishing characteristics, and all the rays together make up the totality of the great source energy.

Ray One has the energy of will and power. It is masculine. Ray Three has the feminine energy of active intelligence. Combining Ray One with Ray Three gives birth to Ray Two, which has the energy of Christ consciousness, or love/wisdom. Since God is comprised of these three major energies, one can say that God is both masculine and feminine. Remember that

God is all that is. God is the source and creator of all that exists. It takes both a father and a mother to create a child. The same holds true for God, creator of all. The only difference is that God is not confined to separate form bodies like we are. His masculine and feminine components are not visible to the human eye because God is spirit; he is a great, powerful energy which is comprised of three major rays of energy that can be further refined as seven rays. Yes, God is both masculine and feminine, or he and she, but to simplify writing this manuscript, I will use the masculine pronouns as I did in the previous sentence. *(Diagram 2 – The Seven Rays)*

By the way, the three major rays are what Christians refer to as the Trinity. The father is Ray One, the son is Ray Two, and the holy spirit/mother is Ray Three.

Diagram 2 – The Seven Rays

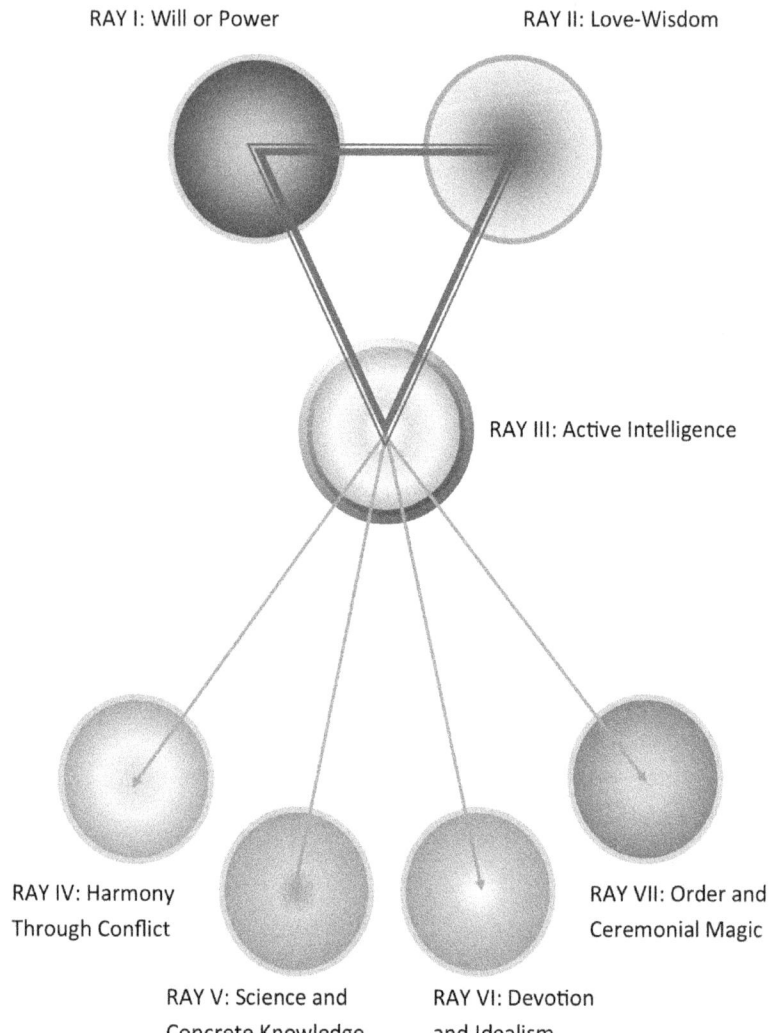

RAY I: Will or Power

RAY II: Love-Wisdom

RAY III: Active Intelligence

RAY IV: Harmony Through Conflict

RAY V: Science and Concrete Knowledge

RAY VI: Devotion and Idealism

RAY VII: Order and Ceremonial Magic

February 26, 2016

Dear Spirit,

Where is all this seven rays and spirit stuff coming from? I have been a Christian all my life and I never heard of these rays in the churches that I attended. Actually, I left my traditional church in order to get answers about mystical experiences that I was having such as: hearing voices, seeing auras and angels, hearing celestial music, seeing clairvoyantly, leaving my physical body and traveling to other planes where I fellowshipped with relatives and friends who had died years ago on the physical plane of earth, and being held and comforted by a spirit being while I was undergoing a major energy shift. I am not Jesus or a holy man in the Bible. I am just an ordinary human being. Please explain why I have had these experiences and why traditional religions did not prepare me for them.

Gratefully yours,

Jackie

February 27, 2016

Spirit Answers:

Wow! This question is loaded! I will begin by addressing the case of the traditional religions. They did not prepare you for your mystical experiences because they could not. Religions teach the interpretation of life at the level of awareness of their founder(s). People are at various levels of consciousness due to the fact that the pace of evolution varies. We are all evolving, but some faster than others. (Jesus, Buddha, and many others were farther ahead in evolution when they lived in dense physical bodies than most earth plane humans are today.) Each religion teaches what the consciousness level of its founder(s) allowed him/them to understand. Can you recall how the Bible passages took on a deeper level of truth when you began your New Thought studies, and an even deeper level of truth when you explored the Ageless Wisdom/Esoteric Philosophy? As one evolves, one is led to seek, and is better able to understand, the varying levels of truth. Or to put it simply, what you believe to be true takes on a deeper meaning as you evolve/grow spiritually. This is because spiritual growth opens channels to greater awareness. When we grow spiritually, we realize, incrementally, that there is much more to the world than what we see and hear on the physical plane of Earth. Much, much more.

The adherents of a religious faith are at an awareness level that allows them to receive and believe the teachings of that religion. In your case, when you began to have mystical experiences, your consciousness level shifted and you began to seek to understand more. At that point, you sought and found teachings that addressed your new level of awareness.

In closing, I must say that you are blessed to have many religions that address people at levels where they are able to understand and receive. That way, no one is left out. For this reason, I believe the Bible is one of the most clever books ever written, because it provides teachings for humans at all levels of consciousness. However, I must caution you that one day, hundreds and maybe thousands of years from now, humanity's consciousness, due to evolution, will exceed the teachings of the Bible, and new teachings will be put in place to guide Earth's humanity. Because life evolves, everything changes. Nothing stays the same.

On parting, I enjoin you to consider that the whole Truth is unknown to any one person or one religion. Only God knows the whole Truth.

My light is dimming so I must go. I will address the other part of your question when we next meet.

March 1, 2016

Spirit Answers:

Jackie, you stated that you are just an ordinary human being and you asked me to explain why you have had mystical experiences. Firstly, let me say that we are all "ordinary human beings"; at least we were all of that classification at one time. In the Bible, Psalm 82:6, and also in John 10:34, Jesus said that we are also Gods.

"Is it not written in your law, 'I said, ye are Gods'?" (ASV)

John 10:34

God is all that is, and we are made in the image of God. Therefore, in potential, we have the qualities that God has. Actually, God expresses through us. We have the power to create all that we want and need. We can express the love of being at one with all that exists. Unfortunately, many Earth dwellers have not come into the level of spiritual development and consciousness to know this as truth. It all goes back to evolution or spiritual growth.

As we evolve in consciousness, we attain the awareness of more and more divine qualities. Some humans begin to hear voices and receive messages that are not coming from Earth's physical plane. Others see little movies or scenes in the third eye, which is in the center of their forehead. Still others feel touches and sensations when no one is physically present to initiate them. Some, like Jesus, begin to heal physical body afflictions with energy from their hands. In addition, beings such as spirit guides, angels, masters, and deceased loved ones become visible and present in the lives of some. These abilities become more pronounced as human beings evolve and progress on the path to becoming spirit beings.

Speaking of the path, there is a definite process to this phenomenon. Just as a baby must go through childhood and adolescence before becoming an adult, all humans progress on a well-defined path of growth before reaching the spirit kingdom, which is the next stage of existence for us. Yes, precious human beings, one day, you will all become spirit beings whose lives are governed by soul consciousness. It's just a matter of time. By knowing this, you can understand more easily what Jesus was trying to teach you. The life of Jesus shows you the path to becoming spirit beings. It shows you the final leg of the path from human being to spirit being. It outlines the initiations that man must undergo in order to gain entrance into the next level of his evolution – the spirit kingdom, also known as the kingdom of souls.

March 1, 2016

Dear Spirit,

You mentioned "initiations" that humans must undergo in order to become spirit beings. Please explain.

Infinite love,

Jackie

March 2, 2016

Spirit Answers:

Ay ay ay ay! Now we're getting deep, which is exactly what I do not want to do in this book. I want to expose people to the truth of who and what they really are and whet their appetites so that hunger and thirst for understanding will lead them to find and read the books that explain this stuff in greater detail. But as I think about it, one cannot understand the true nature of man without knowledge of the aura, the chakras, and the initiations, so I will discuss these subjects briefly.

To understand how man evolves, and why I call it spiritual growth, you must understand that man is made up of levels of energy. Basically, man is an energy, or spirit, being. Each individual has an ovoid body of energy that penetrates and extends out from the form body. We call this body of energy an aura. The aura is made up of different levels of energy consciousness that are linked to the individual by energy vortices that we call chakras. Each chakra controls the inflowing and outpouring of a specific quality of energy into and out of the physical body.

The human aura consists of seven levels of energy. The level closest to the form body is composed of etheric energy, or prana. The other levels consist of physical, astral/emotional, mental, and buddhic/intuitional energies. There are higher vibrational energies also, but we need not concern ourselves with them at this time. *(Diagram 3 – The Human Aura)*

The etheric energy body of the aura is the level which is closest to the physical body. On examining this auric level, one can learn much about the wholeness of the physical body. The colors and the vibration of the energy in the etheric layer of the aura reveal whether the body is functioning in a state of wellness or if there is any area of the body that is functioning below its optimal level. This can show through dark colors and blocked flows of energy, where illness is present. As I mentioned earlier, some people can see the auras of others, and by examining them, they can assess their state of wellness in the physical body. The healing of illness must take place in the energy body in order for an individual to regain wholeness and be cured. Today, many health practitioners treat only the symptoms that are present in the physical body. Consequently, the illness recurs in this or in a future lifetime because it was not eliminated from the energy body.

My light is dimming. I will talk more about this later.

Diagram 3 – The Human Aura

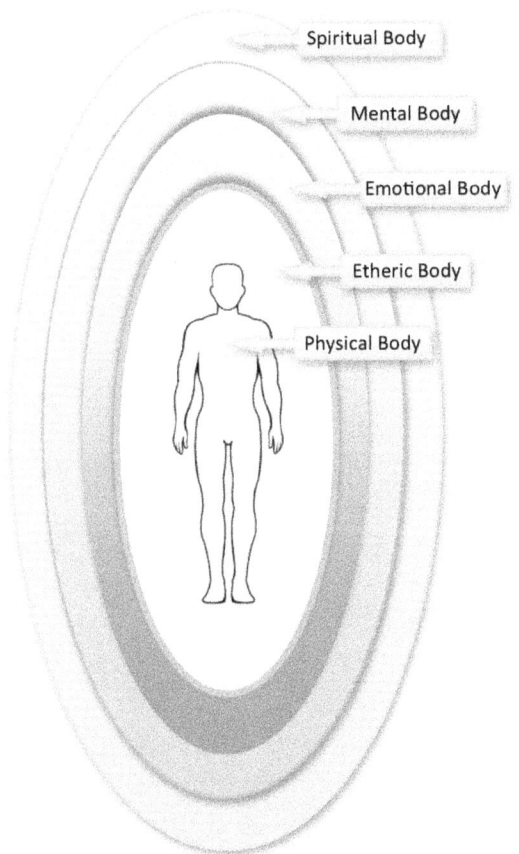

March 3, 2016

Spirit Answers:

Let's talk more about the chakras. As I said earlier, they are vortices that allow energy to flow into the physical body from the outer world via the aura and to flow out from the physical body back into the aura and beyond. If you consider what I just said, you will see that the chakras and auras connect our physical form being to the oneness of all that is. Please think about this.

Previously, I said that the human aura has seven levels of energy. Each level houses a particular kind of energy consciousness. At the present time, the aura of an average human being consists mostly of the etheric body, the emotional body, and some patches of the mental body. As the person grows spiritually, the mental body will develop fully. This will later be followed by the appearance in the aura of a buddhic (intuitional) body and even higher radiations. As the aura expands due to spiritual growth, the individual's contact with the universe expands. In other words, the aura allows the human to communicate with the rest of the universe, or with all that is.

It is important for you to understand how living a virtuous life effects one's aura. Exhibiting positive traits in one's life, such as love, gratitude, honesty, and enthusiasm, helps to protect the aura by attracting energy from a higher vibrational source that increases the aura's atomic substance, also known as soul energy. Positive thoughts, emotions, and actions feed, heal, and protect the aura. One of earth's renowned spiritual teachers, the late Torkom Saraydarian, said that the aura is a "flow of virtues." As virtues outflow from our form being into the aura, the radiation of the aura becomes more magnetic, more colorful, and thus more beautiful. This explains why the various religions all teach us to live virtuous lives. By doing so, we grow spiritually.

You ask: What does this have to do with the chakras? Each chakra permits the flow of a particular level of auric energy into and out of the physical body. The chakras are like bridges that connect the aura and the form body. In other words, they correspond to the energy levels in the aura. For our purposes, we will limit the number of chakras in man to the seven major ones. They are as follows: (1) base of spine, (2) sacral, (3) solar plexus, (4) heart, (5) throat, (6) ajna, and (7) crown. (*Diagrams 4 and 5 – The Seven Chakras*)

My light is dimming fast. I must go. We will continue to talk about the chakras and the initiations later.

Diagram 4 – The Seven Chakras

(Frontal View)

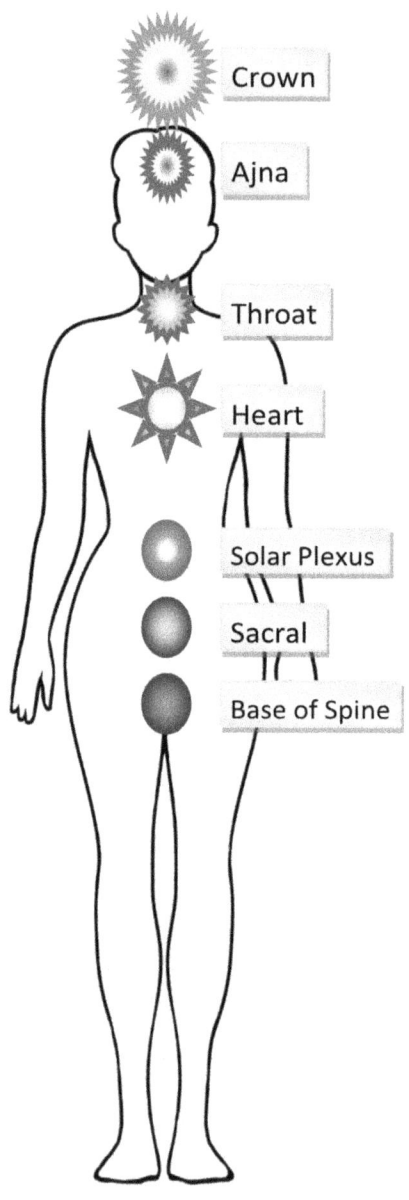

Crown

Ajna

Throat

Heart

Solar Plexus

Sacral

Base of Spine

Diagram 5 – The Seven Chakras

(Side View)

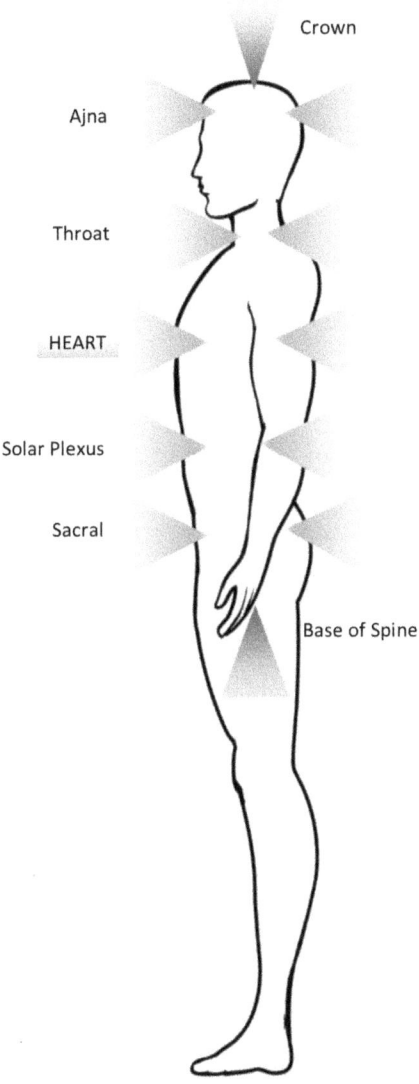

March 4, 2016

Dear Spirit,

I am devastated! I was awake most of last night trying to understand why people are not supporting the spiritual center that I attend. It is one of very few churches in Charlotte that teaches the truth, as I know it. It goes beyond the teachings of New Thought churches and presents smatterings of the Ageless Wisdom. I am so excited that these teachings are being made available to the Charlotte area. Yet, we are struggling. We have lost, and continue to lose, members whose financial support was essential to our well-being. Last night, I read a "resignation from the board of trustees and separation from the spiritual center" letter from a longtime supporter and member. What must we do to survive?

Spirit Answers:

Don't panic, and don't be dismayed. Everything happens for a reason. You know, as well as I know, that in order for your center to survive, you and your current members must believe that it will. You must know in your heart that people who thirst for this level of "knowing" will be attracted to the center, and they will support it financially. Your center is experiencing decline due to one or both of the following:

1. There are not enough people in your locality who are ready to receive the truths as presented in the Ageless Wisdom teachings. I bet the traditional churches in your area are not lacking for membership or money.

2. The prosperity consciousness at your center needs to be raised. If the ministerial staff and board of trustee members do not understand and practice the principles of prosperity, your center will not prosper.

That pretty much sums it up. We can attempt to dissect the personality of the spiritual leaders, the services that are rendered to the members and to the community, the quality of the worship services, etc., but you would be dealing with the symptoms of the illness at your spiritual center rather than the cause. The cause resides in the consciousness of your people. Once this is lifted up, and you allow spirit to guide you, your center will thrive.

This said, let me point out to you that the cure is always to treat the spiritual/energy aspect of an issue. I hope you are beginning to realize that spiritual growth is all about getting our energy bodies in order. This is how we lift our consciousness and eventually become whole again. An understanding of the auras, chakras, and initiations will be helpful to you.

March 8, 2016

Spirit Answers:

Back to the chakras and initiations. Before proceeding to explain the initiations, I must tell you that the energy levels identified in the aura and in the chakras (physical, etheric, astral/emotional, lower mental, higher mental, buddhic, etc.) have corresponding relationships to the systems in the dense physical body. The endocrine glands and the nervous system play major roles in linking the chakras with mechanisms that control the dense form body.

The lower three chakras (base of spine, sacral, and solar plexus) are concerned with the chemical and physical processes of the body whereas the higher three chakras (crown, ajna, and throat) are linked with spiritual and psychological activity. The middle chakra (heart) connects the individual's lower (objective) body with his higher (subjective) one. In other words, it connects his physical and spiritual parts. As one's energy is raised from the base chakra up to the crown chakra, one becomes more and more conscious of his relation to spirit and to all that exists. This process is what I am referring to when I talk about "lifting one's consciousness." It sounds simple, but in reality it takes many, many lifetimes to accomplish this, which leads us to discuss the initiations. That we will do when we next meet.

March 10, 2016

Spirit Answers:

Now let's talk about the initiations. As you now know, man's spiritual development is about expansion of consciousness. As one grows spiritually, he becomes more open to receiving higher, more refined energies into his lower body system. As one receives these higher energies and releases the lower ones that are predominant in humans, one's consciousness is raised. I hope it won't confuse you if I call this higher, more refined energy the Soul, because that is what it is. The Soul is a higher level of consciousness in you. Some refer to it as your higher self *(Diagram 1 – The Three Parts of Man)*. It is a part of your body system, but for many lifetimes we are totally oblivious to its presence. One day, we become aware of it and we begin to earnestly seek God. The entrance of more and more Soul into the lower bodies is a process called soul-infusion. The initiations, when reached, give us an idea of how much soul energy has been infused into the lower energy bodies.

The Esoteric Philosophy presents a system that identifies how much progress one has made on the path of spiritual growth. According to this system, milestones are reached in our spiritual growth when the major activity of energy shifts from one auric level to another (physical to astral/emotional, emotional to lower mental, lower mental to higher mental, higher mental to buddhic). These shifts indicate that the lower body in question has acquired a desired amount of atomic substance, which is another term for soul energy. The lower bodies are becoming soul-infused. For example, when control of the physical body is demonstrated and the emphasis of the individual's activities shift from daily survival (food, clothes, shelter, sex, etc.) to emotional issues, the first initiation has been reached. Similarly, when the control of emotions coupled with control of the physical body is demonstrated, the second initiation is reached. This process continues, but in humans we are concerned with only the first five initiations. When the fourth initiation is reached, man's personality vehicles (physical, emotional and mental) are comprised of 100% higher (atomic) energy and at this point, man enters the next kingdom in nature, which is the spirit kingdom, also called the kingdom of souls. In other words, man becomes a spirit being governed completely by soul consciousness. At this level, man has no need to continue to reincarnate because he has no need of a physical body. He has already reached the state of perfection required in order to enter the spirit kingdom. At the fifth initiation, spirit man becomes a master of wisdom. He leaves the human path and begins a new path of development about which we need not concern ourselves at this time. This is the future that awaits mankind.

So, man is evolving in consciousness from identifying himself as a dense form whose major focus is on the survival of his physical body (food, shelter, clothing, sex) to living largely from his emotions (reacting to life as dictated by anger, lust, greed, sorrow, etc.), to growing and using his lower mental faculties (attaining concrete knowledge), to expanding his mental abilities to understand abstract concepts like the Ageless Wisdom/Esoteric Philosophy, to receiving wisdom intuitively. Since man is an energy being, his evolution leads him from living in a physical body, albeit part-time, to complete liberation from the physical body. Please bear in mind that the whole time when man is residing in a physical body, he is connected to the spirit world via the aura and the chakras. Therefore, God is always with him. Please think about this.

March 12, 2016

Dear Spirit,

Have you been tuning in to the presidential campaign in the United States? Our country is in big trouble, which is reflected in the contention, conflict, and obnoxious behavior present in this campaign. Are we headed into darkness?

Spirit Answers:

Now, now, I believe you are over-reacting. Your country is not really sinking into darkness. I see it as a correction. Your country is taking a giant step in correcting itself so that it can become whole. The conflict, strife, and contention are lifting issues that need to be raised to the surface so that they can be seen clearly and dealt with. It is good that the positions of your two major parties are being spelled out clearly to the public. It is also good that moral issues are being discussed. All of this is good. As for the behavior issues, I must say that they do much in revealing the spiritual maturity level of the candidates and of those who support them.

I do not wish to meddle in the politics of your people, and I certainly will not tell you how to vote. You must vote as your conscience, or rather consciousness, guides you. I will admonish you, however, to heed the teachings on "the middle path" or moderation. I believe positive energies such as love, harmony, peace, and joy result from moderation in one's thoughts, actions, and deeds as opposed to extremism. The world needs positive energies.

I repeat: Don't panic. Everything's going to be fine, sooner or later. The big question is when? Now or many years from now? The pace of the spiritual growth of you and your fellow Americans will determine this because the more you grow spiritually, the higher your consciousness will become. Needless to say, with a high level of consciousness, you will be led to choose leaders whose consciousness level matches or exceeds your own. Again, spiritual growth is the key; it is the solution to every problem.

March 17, 2016

Dear Spirit,

You have mentioned several times that we live many lifetimes. Please explain.

Blessings,

Jackie

March 17, 2016

Spirit Answers:

I can't explain reincarnation without also talking about karma, because they are two pieces that go together. Karma is the spiritual law of cause and effect. It is the law that states that you reap what you sow. What we send out into the Universe is always returned to us. Looking at this on a larger scale, one can say that we are what we have created ourselves to be. This "sending out" originates in the subjective level as ideas and thoughts. It passes from there into our objective lives. For example, before one actually commits murder, he has in his mind the thought of doing so. This process applies to almost everything that happens in our objective life. The idea or thought of it begins at the subjective level of your being, either consciously or subconsciously. This leads us to the New Thought teachings on positive thinking, affirmations and denials, and the role that they play in our spiritual growth, but this is not the place to expound on that. Let me return to the subject at hand, karma and reincarnation.

We have already established that we are spirit beings living in dense physical bodies. We can think of our dense physical bodies as being solidified energy similar to what ice is to water. What we send out in our thoughts and actions becomes attached to us at an energy consciousness level, be it etheric, emotional, mental, or higher levels. In other words, it becomes a part of the appropriate energy level in our aura. If the action or thought produces or adds to the negativity in the world, it becomes a part of the energies of your lower, heavy personality bodies (physical, emotional, mental) and as you know, these energies must be lightened or raised in order for us to grow spiritually. The positive actions or thoughts go directly to the soul consciousness level where they are housed until our lower body energies are all lifted up to that level. Then we ascend (at the fourth initiation) and become spirit beings. This is where the reincarnation piece comes in. The raising of the lower personality body energies is a protracted process. It can take millions of lifetimes. The good news is that most of Earth's humanity, having already evolved through numerous lifetimes, are poised to finish this consciousness raising process in only a few more lifetimes. The exact number of lives left depends on each of you.

Let me back up and explain. Reincarnation is the process of living many lives. When the physical body dies, the real you, which at this point is your soul consciousness, takes with it, via permanent atoms, the energies from the lower personality bodies of the deceased one. They go to an energy plane (astral/emotional, lower mental, or higher mental), whichever coincides with the spiritual growth level of that deceased person, and reside there until the opportunity to enter another physical body and live another lifetime on the Earth plane presents itself. This period of rest between lifetimes varies, but for the average person the rest between lifetimes is from fifty to one hundred years. You are wondering why we come back into physical bodies, aren't you? It's simple. We have to complete our spiritual growth. We lift our energies and raise our consciousness while we are in physical bodies. There is no other way to accomplish this. Therefore, in order to perfect ourselves and have a body system that consists of 100% higher, refined soul energies, we must live in dense bodies and learn much needed lessons. These lessons lead us to work on purifying our lower body system.

The reincarnation piece is rejected by the practitioners of many religions. Yet, I must say that it was fully present in the Bible at one time. This piece was removed from the Bible at an ecumenical council meeting of the Catholic Church in Constantinople in 553 A.D. It is said that the Catholic Church outlawed and put to death those that preached reincarnation. Still, today there are several references in the Bible that are compatible with reincarnation.

For people like you, Jackie, there is no doubt that reincarnation exists because you have made inner plane visits and seen that death was not the end of your loved ones. They are still living beings. In other words, you, like Doubting Thomas in the Bible, have had the proof which erased all doubt. As for those who are not yet convinced, we know that one day soon, when the consciousness of all humanity is lifted, we will all know and accept these teachings as Truth.

March 27, 2016

Dear Spirit,

Everybody talks about prosperity. The goal of everyone is to be rich. What can you tell us about becoming prosperous?

Much gratitude,

Jackie

Spirit Answers:

Guess what. Everyone is rich. Most people just don't know it. God, source and creator of all, provides abundantly for all of His creation. God's abundance is our birthright. Remember the Biblical passage about the lilies in the field? It is true. God provides for the lilies and he also provides for humanity. God provides for all of His creation. He is the source of our supply. There is no lack. There is no scarcity. There is plenty for all of our needs to be met. God's good is unlimited.

How do we tap into the abundance that God provides? Firstly, you must do as the Bible says:

"But seek ye first the kingdom of God, and his righteousness; and all these things shall be added unto you."- (KJV)

Matthew 6:33

By seeking the kingdom, we open our channels and tune into the resources that God provides. We do not just acquire supplies. We must learn to contact and use God's rich supply. Man is limited when he does not allow the Divine within him to express fully. The solution to this, as to all issues, always points to the flow of energy in our lives. The more we raise the vibration of our energy, the easier it is for God's rich supply to flow to us unencumbered. As we progress in growing spiritually, we become less needy, more fulfilled, and more aware that God always provides for his creation.

I will give you some tools that everyone can use to open wider the channels that allow prosperity to flow in one's life:

- Raise your energy vibration.
- Focus on abundance instead of lack, because in reality, there is no lack.
- Be grateful for what you have. If you cannot appreciate what you have, why should God give you more?
- You must state what it is that you want the Universe to provide. "Ask and you shall receive." Making a vision board could be helpful in realizing and organizing your needs and desires.
- Know that whatever you think, feel, say, or do matters in creating your life. Please release all negativity from your life and be positive in all that you say and do.
- Always ask for divine guidance. It is there to help you.
- Be open to accept and follow the divine guidance that you receive.
- Share your riches with others.

I cannot close without commenting more about sharing, for it is the beginning of increasing our financial status. The spiritual law of circulation states that as we give, we receive. We must be generous givers in order to receive abundantly. The Bible teaches us that we should tithe. Tithing is giving ten percent of all that one receives to a person or an organization that is contributing to one's spiritual growth and thus to the spiritual growth of the whole. The act of tithing trains us to be systematic givers and opens the way to systematic receiving. I repeat: As you give, so shall you receive.

Some spiritual leaders teach that tithing is not an option; it is a must. Tithing is a means of thanking God for gifting us with life. God provides generously for us, and we show appreciation for His provisions by sharing with others. We "pay it forward," knowing that our needs will always be met.

In closing, I invite you to use the tools that I have suggested. They have worked for many people, and I strongly believe that they will open the doors to permanent prosperity for you.

April 2, 2016

Dear Spirit,

You have said numerous times that we must raise our consciousness. You explained that raising one's consciousness involves releasing the heavy, negative energies that are in our lower bodies (physical, emotional, and mental) and replacing them with higher, lighter, refined, divine, soul energies. What we are doing is what the Bible refers to as "being born again." We are letting our soul consciousness take dominion over our lower personality consciousness. We are becoming "soul-infused" personalities. How do we accomplish this?

Lovingly yours,

Jackie

Spirit Answers:

I'm glad you asked how one becomes soul-infused and on doing so, takes the fourth initiation, leaves the human kingdom and enters the fifth kingdom, the kingdom of Souls. During the first part of the evolutionary journey, we do nothing consciously because we are not aware that an evolutionary process is taking place in us. We simply exist; we live our lives as best we know how and let evolution run its course. This evolutionary process is very protracted. It has taken eighteen million years to get us to the point where we are now. Fortunately, we are now in an opportune position, for we are poised to make this gigantic shift from human being to spirit being. All cosmic conditions are ripe. The divine, light energies are pouring down on us. All we have to do is open our channels wider and let the energies flow in. How? The Esoteric Philosophy recommends that we meditate, study, and serve.

The *meditation* piece is huge. By meditating, one opens wider the channels that allow the higher energies to flow into the lower personality body. In other words, the source energies (God) become more and more dominant in one's life as one meditates.

I must make it clear that prayer and meditation are not the same although the two can be combined in one process. Prayer is useful when one wants to talk to God. Meditation helps one to become God. I know this statement has raised many eyebrows. I say to you: Calm down! As you receive more and more of the higher, source energies, you become more and more God-like. You put on divine qualities and release lower, base qualities. Eventually, when the course of evolution is run, you return to the Source, which we call God. You become at-one with God. At least, this is how I understand it. I could be wrong because at this point, nobody knows it all. We are all learning, step by step, what the Divine Plan has in store for us. I repeat, nobody, except God, knows it all.

Speaking of knowing and learning, we must study in order to acquire more knowledge. By studying, we open doors and become more aware of this marvelous creation of life. Please don't wait and expect someone else to teach you what you need to know about growing spiritually. Assume that responsibility for yourself and study, study, study. As I stated earlier, there are many books that explain one aspect or another of spiritual growth. They range in readability from primers like this book to much more profound books like Helena Blatvasky's The Secret Doctrine and the series of books written by Alice A. Bailey and the Tibetan disciple Djwal Kul, also known as Master DK. Please find books that match your ability to comprehend and start studying. The more you study, the better you will understand the process of growing spiritually and the sooner you will become receptive to cooperating with this process.

The Ageless Wisdom recommends that we serve in order to grow spiritually. Service means helping others without demanding or expecting compensation. Service can range from helping an elderly person to cross the street, to meditating as a light worker when there is a full moon. When we serve, we open hearts wider. Both the server and the ones served give and receive love. You have probably realized by now that our existence is all about love. The higher, divine energies that we are bringing into our lower personality body are positive energies of love. We are becoming God-like because the energy of God is love.

I would be remiss if I neglected to tell you that some of you will make the shift into the fifth kingdom of nature and become spirit beings without consciously making any effort to do so. You will be "lifted up" by the majority. Some contemporary spiritual leaders are saying that when 51% of Earth humanity's lower energies are transmuted into higher, refined energies, critical mass will be reached and all of Earth's humanity will make the shift of the ages together. You will become, in consciousness, lighter beings. This shift will happen while many of you are still living in physical bodies on planet Earth. This will be the founding of **The New Earth** that is talked about in Revelations, the last book in the Bible. It will be the death of our present age and the birth of a new one. The critical mass event is imminent. It can happen at any time now, be it today, or fifty to one hundred years from now. This will be God's way of assisting us in reaching the fifth kingdom. After all, we have been on this leg of the evolutionary journey for eighteen million years. Isn't it time that we make a giant leap?

April 5, 2016

Dear Spirit,

Every month, people meditate at the time of the full moon. Why?

Light and love,

Jackie

April 5, 2016

Spirit Answers:

If you meditate only one time per month, you will get the greatest benefits if you do it at the time of the full moon. When the moon is full, there is an unimpeded alignment between planet Earth and the Sun. It is believed that the Sun is the energy source for all life on Earth. When the solar energies flow directly to planet Earth, as they do at the time of the full moon, they are powerful and they allow us to approach God, creator of all, unhindered.

Meditating at the time of the full moon offers both individual and group benefits. For the individual, meditation has a purifying effect. The divine energies that are brought down into the lower body are stronger at the time of the full moon and they flush out more negativity from the individual's thoughts, emotions, and energies than would be possible without a full moon. Therefore, the individual's physical, emotional, and mental health is improved. In other words, the individual's consciousness is raised thanks to the spiritual energies that are received during full moon meditations. This makes it easier for the individual to have inner world experiences and to manifest wishes and plans faster.

As for group meditations, the full moon offers great opportunities for world service. Groups of light workers (people of high consciousness and good will) come together, and when they meditate, they become channels to receive and bring down higher, divine energies that they pass on to every living being on Earth. These divine energies can bring healing and peace to others. They also help to raise the consciousness of the masses. Group meditations accelerate the spiritual growth of everyone.

April 6, 2016

Dear Spirit,

I hesitate to ask you how astrology fits into the spiritual development picture because so many people do not want to deal with the astrology piece. They don't understand it, and they don't want to deal with it. I must admit that it is a lot to process. But, considering the major role that it plays in our development, I cannot exclude it from this book. Please explain briefly and simply what astrology has to do with spiritual growth.

Gratefully yours,

Jackie

April 7, 2016

Spirit Answers:

Everything. Astrology has everything to do with the spiritual development of humans. It all goes back to energy. Firstly, we must realize that everything is energy. Therefore, all that exists is in constant movement or vibration. The streams of energy that pass through space relate all celestial bodies and establish the quality and character of all that exists – including the attributes of the personality aspects of human beings. Man's physical, emotional, and mental reactions, his character, and his choices in regards to actions and behaviors, are determined by the energies and forces that act constantly on his personality self and his environment.

Where do these energies come from? They come from the constellations, the stars, the planets, the sun, the moon, the zodiac. In short, they come from all celestial bodies and they effect all of who we are and what we do. That is, they effect the life of the lower personality self of man. As man evolves and comes into soul domination, he is guided more by divine will and less by astrological influences.

There is much more to be explained about the celestial energies and how they shape who we are. The zodiacal energies, in particular, play a huge role in shaping the character of man. Each month, when a particular zodiacal sign is in force (full moon), and we admit those energies into our personality body (meditation), we are admitting the qualities that that sign houses. Since the energies of our dense personality body are heavy, we draw forth, at first, the base qualities of the zodiacal sign. As we grow spiritually, we draw forth lighter qualities. For example, the vain, self-centered leonine base qualities become heart-centered, generous soul qualities.

Having been warned to keep this explanation brief and sweet, I will stop at this point and refer those who wish to learn more about astrology's connection to spiritual growth to the books that expound on this topic. On leaving, I implore you to consider all that I have said about energy:

All is energy, including God. God is source energy, creator of all that is. Energy is in constant movement. Energies interrelate with other energies, including man and they effect constant change. Everything is evolving. Change is inevitable. Everything must change. Nothing stays the same.

Are you seeing the larger picture more clearly?

April 8, 2016

Dear Spirit,

Earth's humanity deals with multiple challenges. Racism seems to be ongoing, and addictions are at an all-time high. There are heated differences of opinion in regards to abortion, homosexuality, and transgender and bisexual proclivities. The poverty rate is soaring and obesity is rising. How do we overcome these and other challenges that plague us?

Your humble servant,

Jackie

April 9, 2016

Spirit Answers:

Humanity is embodied on Earth to learn. We are learning how to cooperate with the forces of evolution and become co-creators with God. Unfortunately, the majority of Earth's humans learn through pain and suffering. We have to hit rock bottom before becoming receptive to a painless way of living.

The challenges that humanity deals with are always painful. People are murdered, judged, and scorned. People die due to lack of proper nutrition and healthcare. People terrorize others due to jealousy and differences of opinion as to how life should be lived on this planet. The list goes on.

Our job is to work through these challenges and resolve them peacefully and harmoniously. We are trying, but we have not yet succeeded, because we are seeing and understanding our life issues with our physical plane outer eyes and our lower personality consciousness. We do not understand these challenges from a spiritual perspective, because if we did, they would not be considered as challenges, and they certainly would not be painful.

Seeing with spiritual eyes and understanding with divine consciousness, we would know that we cannot dictate how people must be, nor should we try to change them. No fourth kingdom human being is perfect. What we label as perfection comes in man upon graduating into the fifth kingdom, the kingdom of souls. When we become spirit beings and reside in the fifth kingdom, we are free of all lower, negative energies and the problems that stem from them. Since we all still reside on the physical plane as human beings, no one should judge or scorn another's perceived imperfections.

Furthermore, with divine consciousness, we understand that there is no right or wrong. These are man's labels, not God's. Whatever is, just is. If it causes us discomfort, we can change it by adjusting the vibration of our energy. If our energy vibrates with love and harmony, all is well. Instead of judging others and dictating how they must be, our divine reaction would be to LOVE them. Love them exactly as they are, and let them be, for we know that God is in control and in time we will all be totally God-like.

In case you haven't realized it yet, the key to eliminating life's challenges is to raise our consciousness. We must grow spiritually. On doing so, everyone will reside in an ambiance of love. Everyone will see himself in all others. We will all know that we are ONE, and we will relate to each other lovingly and respectfully. We will share with one another, for greed will no longer exist. We will not suffer bodily ailments, because our dense physical bodies will no longer exist; they will be spiritualized light bodies. This New Earth, populated by spirit beings, will be our paradise. This is why we must "seek ye first the kingdom of God, and his righteousness."- (KJV) By inheriting the kingdom, we shed all pain and suffering and we eliminate all earthly challenges.

April 11, 2016

Dear Spirit,

I do not have any more questions to ask you at this time. Are there any concluding remarks that you would like to make?

With much gratitude,

Jackie

April 12, 2016

Spirit Answers:

I thank you for giving me this opportunity to teach. It is very important that humanity progress on the evolutionary journey, and in order to do so, human beings must raise their consciousness. The personality self must be purified and changed into a higher grade of energy. The spirit entities in the higher world are helping Earth's humanity by providing myriad activities of light. Please know that you are not alone. We love you, and we hope to welcome you soon to your new way of being.

To be blunt, the higher energy frequencies, in which the kingdom of souls has residence, cannot support the lower, negative energies in which the human kingdom now resides. You must raise these energies in order to make the shift into the next kingdom. The kingdom of souls, which is void of lower energies, is "heaven" to human beings. There is no aging, death, disease, or poverty. Racism, prejudice, greed, jealously, and pride are not present in the fifth kingdom. Everyone is loved, and all needs are provided for. The consciousness is no longer focused on the individual. The group, the whole, is all-important because everyone knows that we are all ONE.

The question is: Now or Later? Do we work with our spirit guidance and accelerate our spiritual growth process, or do we ignore spirit and continue on the slower, scenic route? The destination is the same either way, and we will reach this destination, for our victory is assured. At least, the higher world believes that it is. The question remains: When?

One of the ascended masters of wisdom, Master Morya, asked the following question: *"Why a thousand lives, when ten will do?"*

Now I am asking you: Will you live a thousand or more lifetimes, or will you make the shift from the *human kingdom to the kingdom of souls* in ten lifetimes or fewer? It's up to you.

Thank you for reading my words. I bid you farewell.

Your Spirit Co-Author

ABOUT THE AUTHOR

Jacqueline Louise McNeil Watts was born in Charlotte, North Carolina. She is the middle child of seven babies born to Samuel and Mary McNeil. Jackie and her siblings (Ann, Frankie, Joyce, Patricia, Shelia, and Samuel, Jr.) were raised in a traditional Baptist church where they were taught Christian values.

After graduating from Knoxville College in Knoxville, Tennessee, with a bachelor degree in education, Jackie taught French and Spanish in the Columbus, Ohio, public school system. During her thirty-six years of service with Columbus Public Schools, Jackie earned a master's degree in foreign language education from The Ohio State University; taught French in Columbus high schools for twenty-nine years; taught English as a foreign language in a high school in Luang Prabang, Laos, for one year (Fulbright Grant); served full-time as a PAR (Peer Assistant and Review) consultant for first-year teachers and veteran teachers who were in need of intervention; and served as a retired teacher on special assignment to the deputy superintendent of the Columbus school system. During this time, Jackie was a very active member of United Methodist churches in Columbus.

In 1985, Jackie was devastated when her mother suffered and died from colon cancer. Her father had just passed in 1984. Jackie's grief was intense; she was inconsolable. She became deeply depressed. Spirit stepped in and rescued Jackie.

Her depression disappeared instantly when she heard Spirit say: "I assure you, you will be all right." Ironically, it was said in French!

After this occurrence, Jackie began to pay attention to the mystical phenomena that were taking place in her life. It seemed that the more she focused on them (through meditation, service, and study), the more prevalent they became. Seeking understanding of these mystical experiences, Jackie began studying Spiritualism, followed by New Thought, and later Ageless Wisdom/Esoteric Philosophy. Today, she continues to study the New Thought and Ageless Wisdom teachings, and she stays updated on humanity's evolutionary progress by receiving the teachings of highly evolved contemporary spiritual teachers. Jackie participates regularly in an Esoteric Philosophy study group, a full moon meditation group, and a meditation group that meets weekly at Piedmont Unitarian Universalist Church. She embraces the social activism platform of the Unitarians and she provides additional service to humanity through two civic and service national organizations of which she is an active member: Alpha Kappa Alpha Sorority, Inc., and Chums, Inc.

In 2012, Jackie moved back to Charlotte, North Carolina, where she is surrounded by family and friends. In 2016, she wrote and had published Spirit Answers *(A Primer to Understanding Spiritual Growth)*. Jackie's mission is to share with others what she has learned while consciously treading the path of spiritual growth. Her life has been a roller coaster ride, but as the "Happy Goodmans" Gospel Family would sing in their well-known song: *She wouldn't take nothing for her journey now.*